SUFFERING

A Caregiver's Guide

SUFFERING
A Caregiver's Guide

John L. Maes

ABINGDON PRESS
Nashville

SUFFERING: A CAREGIVER'S GUIDE

Copyright © 1990 by Abingdon Press

This book is printed on acid-free paper.

Library of Congress Cataloging-in-Publication Data

Maes, John L., 1923–
  Suffering: a caregiver's guide / John L. Maes.
    p.   cm.
  Includes bibliographical references.
  ISBN 0-687-40570-X (alk. paper)
    1. Suffering 2. Suffering—Religious aspects—Christianity. 3. Consolation. I. Title.
BF789.78.M24   1990
233—dc20

                                  89-27485
                                    CIP

MANUFACTURED IN THE UNITED STATES OF AMERICA

This book is dedicated to those I can never forget: to Barbara, for irreplaceable memories; to my father, who opened up a world of possibilities for his family in the new world; to Aunt Betty, who retained grace and beauty while dying; to Albert Danielsen, who framed the work of caregivers with his vision and gifts; and to Mary, still very much alive, who has seen and shared it all with consummate warmth and courage.

* * *

I want also to acknowledge Charles Kao, who stimulated the idea for the book; Chris Schlauch, who meticulously read the entire manuscript; Richard Kahn, who struggled through "The Many Faces of Suffering"; and my irrepressible editor, Greg Michael. Not to be forgotten are the many hours of careful and thoughtful copyediting provided by Steve Cox, whose work was important in bringing this book into being. All these friends challenged and criticized my writing, but always with respect and encouragement and to them I offer deep appreciation and thanks. Their contributions have enhanced the quality of the writing as well as my own self-esteem. Their gifts of time, penetrating intelligence, and regard for the subject matter were invaluable.

Contents

CONTENTS

Preface

Nineteen seventy-five was the watershed year in my life. Before that, issues like promotion, tenure, and professional credibility were much more important to me. I engaged myself in writing that showed off intellectual facility, set up clever paradigms, and addressed them with nifty intellectual footwork. The effort was exhilarating, and the academic community was very good to me.

In 1975 my father and my daughter died. My father was a Flemish Belgian immigrant who rode in steerage to Ellis Island at the age of ten. Inside that shaved-headed, frightened boy was a man who set the table for his whole family in America. He died from cancer of the colon at the age of seventy-two, a respected, reasonably affluent man, well known for his strength and integrity. My heart is filled with respect and gratitude whenever I think of him.

My father died in October at the end of his long illness. We had time to say good-bye and sit through the death watch together. This slow and steady mastery of bereavement was interrupted without warning in March of 1975. Our thirty-one-year-old daughter, Barbara, died suddenly, of a pulmonary embolism. She left her husband and three little girls: twins seven years old and another daughter fourteen months younger. I have written of this terrible experience in a chapter titled "Loss and Grief in Fathering" in a book called

Fathering: Fact or Fable? (edited by Edward V. Stein, published by Abingdon in 1977).

Since that time my life has changed. Concerns about job security no longer seem weighty. I have always tried to make the world a better place for myself and others, but this intention has been much more focused since our daughter died. I have accepted the fact that my professional life is primarily a vehicle for caring rather than an arena for ambition and success. The forty years I have been a pastor, psychotherapist, supervisor, professor, director, and dean have all been fired by the same underlying motive: to help heal myself and others from the sufferings and sorrows of life. Since 1975 my interest in professional literature has moved toward writings with greater human scope and existential depth.

This book was written from the inside out. It began with the need to make meaning of traumatic events in my own life. In addition to the grief of great losses, the death of these two greatly loved persons opened up the history of my being an immigrant's kid. The feeling of being "dumb," unstylish, and outside the social in-group had not been overcome by successes. A reworking of my system of self-esteem was required. My ontological security was at stake. Religious faith and deep human relationships have been the most helpful antidotes to the pervading sense of inferiority that threatens a person with my background. Perhaps that is why persons like me are attracted to "great causes." The great cause for me has been sharing the secret of the love of God, first through preaching and evangelism, later through pastoral care, and finally through pastoral psychotherapy. When I remember how little I knew when I began, I am grateful for the deepened sense of integrity, competence, and compassion that have grown through the years. I believe I have led the way in building structures for the training of professional caregivers; now it is time to share some of what I have learned. My work has been a way to express my gratitude to God for sustaining me through sorrow and alienation, helping me grow toward the bright promise of full humanness.

So, this book is an effort to make sense of suffering: to understand my own and to respond to that of others. I hope to provide a unique perspective on suffering, one that has developed through years of experience as a professional caregiver. Although the readers most like myself will be ministers and psychotherapists, there are others who do the work of caring and healing who may find this perspective meaningful as well. I hope the book will also be read by sufferers. I hope they will discover that the "languages" used do not separate me from their experience, but are only ways of talking about what we share so deeply.

As the book progresses, the languages of existential philosophy, practical theology, and clinical description will be used as major frames of reference. In our attempt to understand such a universal phenomenon as suffering, several more kinds of discourse will be called upon. These will reflect the various situations within which human suffering occurs. So at times the writing may seem more psychological, physiological, sociological, or theological than at other times. The character of suffering and its location within human experience will determine the terms used.

It seems we all must suffer and we must try to make sense of our suffering, for we are vulnerable, meaning-making creatures. Although there is always room for mystery and puzzlement in our lives, not to make sense is not to be sane. Suffering tests the limits of meaning-making, but there are certain social contexts, relationships, and perspectives that help most when life is painful and confusing. It is in search of these that this effort has been launched.

In the first chapter, puzzling questions are raised about the nature of suffering. The responses to these questions lead to a definition of suffering. The second chapter attempts to communicate the special qualities of suffering and to frame the contexts that affect its intensity and direction. The third chapter presents a number of the appearances that suffering assumes and the arenas within which responses are acted out. These three chapters present the case of the sufferer.

From the fourth chapter on, the book relates itself more fully to the caregiver's view of the sufferer. This includes examples of recovery from suffering and despair, and some cautions and suggestions to help caregivers in their tasks. The last chapter deals with both the importance and the difficulty of finding meaning in the midst of suffering. It recognizes that some of the causes of suffering are the result of political oppression or "acts of God," which especially challenge the sufferer's ability to make sense of what is happening. The need to make meaning cannot be avoided no matter how overwhelming the circumstances; thus, we conclude by discussing the necessary conditions for this difficult task.

Since suffering and despair are essentially spiritual problems, the efforts toward the understanding and healing of sufferers are framed within my belief that healing and growth occur within and ultimately because of divine grace. So, while this book is at times analytical, at times theological or philosophical, it is at all times a witness to the source of healing in all our lives. I have shared with you in many ways: my thinking, my professional experience, the healed wounds of my own suffering, the joy and challenge of caregiving, and the stories of clients who were willing to share their lives with you. My effort is not so much to convince as to share and model; not so much to give answers as to make sense of suffering—to act as a living bridge between you and other sufferers.

I have tried to use inclusive, rather than sexist, language. Quotations have been rendered faithful to the original however, and may include such language. When this occurs the reader may share my discomfort with the decision (and obligation) to respect the integrity of the original.

CHAPTER ONE

The Nature of Suffering

One day I sat working in a quiet office amid the sleeping quarters of a mental hospital ward. I was writing evaluation reports and summarizing patient interviews. All the patients in this forty-bed ward were in the dayroom along with the rest of the staff, except for one patient whom I shall call Tom. Diagnosed as having a schizo-affective disorder, Tom was confined to a seclusion room near the office where I was working. Because he was in such a state of intense agitation there appeared to be danger that he might injure himself. As the long afternoon sun filtered through the windows of the normally quiet area the silence was periodically broken by incredible cries of pain and terror: "Oh God, I'll give you anything if you make them stop shooting me!" Who or what those unknown torturers may have been remains a mystery to this day, but the intensity of the pain and terror lingers on in my memory after thirty years.

This incident, describing the behavior of a young man whose emotional illness may seem to be rare, unique, bizarre, and distant from our "normal" experience, disturbs us and raises important questions about the nature of suffering. These questions, and the development of thoughtful responses to them, provide a deepened understanding of suffering for those of us who suffer and those of us who minister to sufferers.

Key Questions About the Nature of Suffering

Tom's story presents us with a difficult puzzle. There was no objective physical danger. The room was empty, except for a mattress on the floor. He appeared to be in good physical health and was not visibly harming himself; and, of course, no one was really shooting him. Yet, his cries of agony were accompanied by obvious signs of agitation. He paced the floor with his distorted face streaked with tears, all the while wringing his hands as he cried out. If there was no physical danger, what caused his repeated outbursts of emotional pain? What was the source of his terror? Why were his perceptions so different from "objective" reality? Where lies the dividing line between the objective world and one's perceptions? Which is reality?

Tom's story tells us that in intense suffering, perception becomes the only reality. But perception may seriously distort objective reality. This is important, because a bridge to objective reality may be the only route to healing.

The early writings of Gestalt psychology help to further focus this question. Kurt Koffka once recounted an old German legend that told the story of a man who rode his horse across Lake Constance in the midst of a terrible blizzard. After an interminable journey he finally saw the lights of an inn on the shore. Not knowing where he was or where he had been, he pounded on the door. The innkeeper opened the door to see a stranger rimed with snow and ice. As Koffka told the story, the innkeeper "in a tone of awe and wonder," said: "Do you know that you have ridden across the Lake of Constance?" At which the rider dropped stone dead at his feet.[1] There had been a shift in the rider's perception of reality, so dramatic that it caused his death. Although his perception of the world may have been illusory, his death was real. (In the practice of voodoo, it is believed that such shifts in perception often cause death.)

Koffka used this illustration to demonstrate the relationship between the physical field and the psychological field of the perceiver, correctly pointing out that the psychological field is the primary "reality" to which the person responds.

This can be seen clearly in the case of Tom's perceptions described above. To Tom the physical and emotional discomfort were real. If there were no objective evidences of harm or danger, what caused Tom to experience them?

The experience of suffering was obviously intensified by mental images that were interpreted, or "seen" by Tom, as being deadly. Although Tom's words give us some insight to the images that were keeping the intense suffering alive, only he will ever know who or what creatures of his own imagination were attacking him. The shape, movement, and coloration of those figures, whether they were human, humanoid, or otherwise will remain forever within the secret domain of his terror.

Tom's projections were triggered by what learning theorists call "mediating variables."[2] These consist of thoughts and images which may have been stored in the brain as memories for years. Yet under certain conditions, they can stimulate powerful emotional responses just as surely as if they were real objects in the environment of the person. To avoid confusion over the problem of "reality" in this context, Freud simply referred to thoughts, images, and "real" things equally as objects that can create terror.[3] Tom's suffering would not have been greater had he been attacked by real persons with real instruments of destruction. In fact, a real attack might have caused less suffering, since he would have had a better sense of how to respond. Perception was reality for Tom, as it is for all sufferers, and his tenuous bridge to objective reality made it almost impossible for him to change that perception.

What Is Reality?

Fixed and permanent objects or everyday concerns and events are most likely to be defined as real by society as a whole. These are examples of what I call "consensual reality." Such objects and events are relatively easy to point at, or to agree on. However, each person's sense of objective "reality" is affected by thoughts and images which have the emotional power to temper or intensify perceptions and experiences, including experiences of suffering. Especially during periods of stress there is a tendency to "bend" reality in the direction of subjective experience. Therefore, what may cause some persons to suffer does not similarly affect others, because of the differences in their perceptions of reality.

A statement from Dietrich Bonhoeffer in one of his letters from Tegel prison in Berlin illustrates this point:

This is my second passiontide here. People sometimes suggest in their letters that I am suffering here. Personally, I shrink from such a thought, for it seems a profanation of that word. . . . Of course, there's a good deal here that's appalling, but isn't it the same everywhere? Perhaps we have tended to exaggerate the whole question of suffering, and have been too solemn about it . . . . I believe for instance that all real suffering contains an element of physical pain. We are always too inclined to emphasize the sufferings of the soul. Yet that is just what Christ is supposed to have removed from us . . . . I am sure we need a good deal of correction on this point.[4]

Bonhoeffer's courageous statement presents a uniquely limited definition of suffering. For most persons, situations like the Holocaust are loaded with emotional terror and somatic pain and thus are almost guaranteed to cause suffering. The fact that he did not consider himself to be suffering is evidence that subjective interpretations may determine the presence of and intensity of suffering.

Bonhoeffer's statement "I believe for instance that all real suffering contains an element of physical pain"[5] raises two further important questions for our consideration: What are the relationships between the subjective and objective elements of suffering? And what are the relationships between physical pain and suffering?

Subjective and Objective Elements of Suffering

In psychological terms Tom was suffering from a mental illness diagnosed as a schizo-affective disorder. In Tom's case this illness included a mood disorder, with both manic and depressive features, along with a severe thought disturbance, which included his delusions and hallucinations of being attacked. A modern case analysis would likely have revealed a troubled childhood with such traumatic events as death in the family, divorce, alcoholic parents, or other interferences with the development of object relationships. In all likelihood, more recent social stressors had been the immediate triggers for Tom's problems.

Today we would expect to find neurological malfunctions in his brain caused by a combination of genetics, developmental history, and anxiety. These would probably be treated with medication. But this plausible explanation fails to express the experiential quality of Tom's suffering. Such words as *terror, pain, agitation, apprehension,* and *confusion* come to mind only when we consider his personal suffering. These words remind us that suffering must be understood in light of the subjectivity of the sufferer. Compare the quality of the following famous words to the objective description above:

Terrors are turned upon me; they pursue my soul as the wind: and my welfare passeth away as a cloud.
And now my soul is poured out upon me; the days of affliction have taken hold upon me.
My bones are pierced in me in the night season; and my sinews take no rest.
By the great force of my disease is my garment changed; it bindeth me about as the collar of my coat.
He hath cast me into the mire, and I am become like dust and ashes.
(Job 30:15-19 KJV)

How much closer this ancient description of Job's agony seems to Tom's suffering than the clinical description given above. Human suffering, including our own, is better understood in subjective terms. It is this subjective understanding that creates the empathy necessary for effective pastoral care, psychotherapy, or medical healing to take place.

What Are the Relationships Between Pain and Suffering?

Though they frequently occur together, suffering and pain are not the same. For our purposes, pain will be seen as physically related, less general in scope, and usually shorter in duration than suffering. An example of pain is a localized physical discomfort associated with a bodily disorder, disease, or injury.

Suffering will refer to intense mental or emotional distress of longer duration, arising from a complex of causes that may include physical pain. Examples of suffering include bereavement, depression, anxiety states, physical disability, and economic losses.

Since Bonhoeffer was not in physical pain, he believed that his suffering was less than that of others. However, the relationship between pain and suffering is more complicated than Bonhoeffer's statement implies. Physical pain is often a trigger for suffering, but it is not a necessary condition in itself. The history of psychology reveals some unusual events with regard to experiencing pain.

During the first half of the nineteenth century in Europe, Mesmerism was developed and proposed to the world by Friedrich Anton Mesmer.[6] Beginning with the theory that energy could be transmitted to persons by passing magnets over their bodies, he demonstrated cures for neuroses and other illnesses. Eventually Mesmer became aware that the magnets he used to effect the "animal magnetism" in his patients were unnecessary. He could simply move his hands over his patients and create remarkable cures. It was suggestion, not magnetism, that was being transmitted. This led to the discovery and use of hypnotism as a cure for what we now call conversion hysterias, for example, paralyses or anesthesias for which there is no "physical" cause. It also led to the use of hypnotism as an anesthetic.

By the mid–nineteenth century, James Esdaille was running a hospital in India using hypnosis as the anesthetic in major operations. This technique spread to England, where, in 1842, W. S. Ward removed a leg using a mesmeric trance and reported to the Royal Medical and Chirurgical Society that the patient experienced no pain.[7]

From Bonhoeffer we learned that conditions which cause intense pain and suffering for some persons are not perceived to cause suffering by others. Religious faith and the ability to depersonalize terrible circumstances appear to provide a buffer against suffering. Hypnosis demonstrated that attention can be focused away from normally traumatic physical events so that there is no experience of pain. Both religion and hypnosis, it seems, can mitigate experiences of pain and suffering, yet if mental and emotional states can diminish the experience of pain, they can also intensify it.

Physical pain was not a major cause of Tom's suffering. Although I am convinced that Tom was experiencing intense physical pain, I am equally convinced that it was as a result of his suffering. Sleeplessness, headaches, burning eyelids, muscle tension, even neuralgic involvements can be the results of what we call emotional problems and thus become part of suffering without having been the initial triggers for suffering. So, while physical pain is usually present with suffering, it is often a result rather than a cause.

Overarching in all of the above examples is the impact of the person's "mental" or emotional state. If we are to understand the meaning of suffering and how to minister effectively to sufferers, we must look beyond physical causes and physical pain to the emotional conditions. And if we are to understand these emotional conditions we must look beyond them to the belief and value structures that determine one's perceptions and interpretations of experience.

Is Suffering Always Interpersonal?

Earlier I noted that Tom spent the afternoon pleading with God to "make them stop shooting me." Although we do not know who "they" were, "they" were obviously important figures in Tom's phantasmagoric perceptual world. Thus, Tom's tragic dilemma raises still another question in one's mind: Does suffering always have an interpersonal context no matter how solitary it may seem to be?

Harry Stack Sullivan, author of *The Interpersonal Theory of Psychiatry*, states that all behavior is ultimately interpersonal. Although basic biological behaviors are initially driven by "safety needs," such as the need for food, water, warmth, and so on, they soon become conditioned to such needs as holding, communication, approval, and acceptance. Sullivan called these latter needs "security" needs. Thus, he concludes that the need for significant others is at the center of personality organization, with loneliness being the most terrible early experience.[8]

If this intense interpersonal need cannot be met by reaching over our loneliness to make human contact, an imagined community may be fabricated through projected mental images to people one's lonely world. In this schizoid manner, Tom's fearful tormentors may have been part of his attempt to overcome his unbearable sense of being alone in his suffering. One can imagine that Tom, unable to bear the weight of human interaction and responsibility, unable to be appropriately close to others, still chose to fill his world of madness with human-like creatures. It is possible that even these maddened relationships were more tolerable than complete aloneness. This would support the thesis that suffering is always interpersonal for human beings, that at the core of suffering is the sense of being cut off from normal human relationships. Therefore, the greatest pain in suffering may be the loneliness.

The Sufferer and God

Tom raised another issue important to our understanding of suffering when he said, "Oh God, I'll give you anything if you make them stop shooting me!" Pressed to his existential limits by suffering, he spoke to God. He spoke to God either as archetypal parent or as Ultimate Being; and in doing so, he could have been speaking for all of us.

Are not our inner desires to grow, to be better, wiser, and kinder, silently spoken to someone beyond ourselves? Is there not a voice that silently speaks in all of us, saying to our God, "I'll be good if you . . . ," "I'll do better if only you . . . "? And is this not true regardless of the nature of our theology or the level of our religious development? Is this not true even if God is not named, or identified in our "prayer" with that beyond ourselves?

Tom's cries cause us to ask whether all suffering is spiritual in nature. We may assume, both from our experience and from the discussion above, that suffering requires self-consciousness and that it is interpersonal. But does it also require a sense of relationship to a higher or ultimate being? If so, then it is against this backdrop of ultimate power and mystery that the drama of our suffering is played out. Is this what makes the spiritual elements of hope and despair so crucial to an understanding of suffering? Certainly the most pathos-filled words recorded of Jesus on the cross are to be found in Mark 15:34 (RSV):

And at the ninth hour Jesus cried with a loud voice, "Eloi, Eloi, lama sabachthani?" which means, "My God, my God, why hast thou forsaken me?"

It was not the physical pain, the social isolation, or the mockery and rejection that were the most painful, but the sense of alienation from God. I propose that this sense of alienation from Ultimate Being, from cosmological rootedness, is the cause of the despair that lies at the core of suffering. Regardless of one's interpretation of this source of "ultimate meaning," whether it be God in the Freudian sense of projected superparent, or in the Tillichian sense of Ultimate Being, it lies at the core of one's interpretation of life. And this is equally true whether one formalizes the idea of God as being at the center of life or not.

Suffering and the Limits of Human Existence

Suffering often occurs at our existential limits. Death and loss, ennui, and the fear of nonbeing are terms we associate with suffering. Yet such limits can also be occasions for joy. Events such as birth and death have great possibilities for both. So do opportunities that have the potential for great successes and failures.

The very scope of human existential awareness permits joy and suffering beyond the normal animal limits of any other creature. The incredible existential potential within which human beings live was expressed by Ernest Becker in these words:

She [nature] created an animal who has no defense against full perception of the external world, an animal completely open to experience. . . . He can relate not only to animals in his own species, but in some ways to all other species. He can contemplate not only what is edible for him, but everything that grows. He not only lives in this moment, but expands his inner self to yesterday, his curiosity to centuries ago, his fears to five billion years from now when the sun will cool, his hopes to an eternity from now.[9]

Perhaps the magnitude and intensity of suffering can only be understood within such an incredible context and upon such a grand stage. Unique among all creatures, human beings have self-consciousness, a sense of the limits and possibilities of their own existence, a sense of the magnitude of the universe in which they exist, and at least a projected sense of their own importance in the mind of God. It is this bittersweet mix of limitation and specialness that answers to Bonhoeffer's demurrer and recognizes both the personal and cosmic importance of human suffering. It is not normal to be as above the conditions for human suffering as Bonhoeffer seemed to be. We read his letters with great respect and admiration. Yet reading those letters is sometimes similar to engaging in therapy with a person who has developed a defensive barrier against his or her own emotions. You hear the tragic story of a life, hurting inside, while waiting for the storyteller to manifest appropriate affect. You keep saying to yourself, "Where is the feeling?"

Given the sense of personal specialness and cosmic awesomeness we all seem to share, it is understandable that personal calamities such as physical injury, the loss of loved ones, and career failures become magnified into events of cosmic significance. Tom stands at one end of the human continuum, aggrandizing his personal fears and anxieties into gargantuan struggles of cosmic proportions. Dietrich Bonhoeffer stands at the other, a self-transcending giant, modeling moral greatness in the midst of truly catastrophic circumstance. And the rest of us are in between, living in the most integrated and effective style we can manage, with a quiet sense of dread beneath our confident demeanors, only occasionally having our dread-filled energy focused in suffering.

Stanislas Breton has added further insight into the existential nature of suffering:

Suffering, whatever be the specific modality which a form gives it, is the sign in us of that power of the world dispersed in an infinity of dangers. It is that which makes of the other and the opponent the undesirable guest who makes himself at home with us. The "to suffer" then takes on a new inflection. It passes from the indetermination which anticipates the universal danger to the burdensome reality of an evil, a sickness, an "in spite of us" to which medical terminology gives a more or less precise name. It has often been said that there are sick people and not sicknesses.[10]

Thus, in suffering, the existential anxiety that haunts all creatures made vulnerable by their awareness of the panoramic universe—the specialness of their own existence and the brevity of life—becomes focused in feared reality. In suffering, the dreaded fear of being overwhelmed is finally at the door.

Suffering and Meaning

The relationship between suffering and meaning is of particular importance to this discussion. No matter what the cost, a person will try to find meaning in suffering. Tom's frantic efforts to organize his world resulted in idiosyncratic, bizarre ideas and behavior. But that behavior supports the proposition often made by mental-health workers, that thought disorders are attempts to organize human experience in the only ways that seem meaningful under the circumstances. For example, a paranoid person might give meaning to his or her irrational suspicions by believing that a heinous international cabal had been formed to discover and steal his or her secrets.

All intelligent people, when struck with life-threatening illness, sudden loss of loved ones, or unexpected business failures struggle to put these strange and threatening events into some kind of meaningful context. It may be that suffering is most intense when a convincing context simply cannot be devised. It is then that we hear from sufferers about the unjustness of life, the insensitivity of others, the good fortune of others, and the "why me?" complaints. We may assume that the need for meaning lies at the core of our experience and that both understanding and predictability, the essentials for sanity, depend on it.

But being able to explain things is not enough. We must have faith in meaning, especially when circumstances are temporarily unexplainable. Belief in meaning holds us when the picture is incomplete through lack of experience, data, or philosophical or scientific sophistication. It holds us when the circumstances of our lives are chaotic, when we are overwhelmed by losses or failures, when we are suddenly taken ill. Since we can never "know" enough to be completely safe, we substitute belief in meaning for data. Monroe amplifies this idea:

That which has become meaningful for us through intentional acts might be compared by analogy to a mere nutshell floating on a fathomless and tumultuous sea. But this tumultuous sea, still meaningless to us, is not empty of meaning. It has a still hidden and unspoken meaning which Strasser refers to as "premeaning" or "fundamental meaning," in contradistinction to the "signified" meaning which has already revealed itself through our discovering acts. There is an element of dread in this vague premeaning, which seems to be a basic human condition. Those who cannot accept this dread, according to Tillich, deny this mystery by substituting a false certitude, often in the form of neurotic, particularly obsessive behavior. The obsessional individual refuses to accept the mystery of this ontological truth.[11]

Thus we are faced with the need for meaningful organization of life experience; the need to believe that all experience can potentially be organized; and the continuous underlying dread that we may not be able to manage this and that life will become chaotic and unexplainable. This subtle dread is one of the important elements in suffering.

It is difficult to explain all of life's events in ordinary times, but explaining them becomes impossible to accomplish in times of crisis, grief, or "acts of God." Therefore, we are all driven to belief in meaning; that is, to faith. People have faith in God, the future of science, communism, astrology, the direction of evolution, the ultimate goodness of humankind, in short, in some kind of formula that helps them make sense of their existence. The lack of a sustaining sense of meaning leads to confusion and suffering. Tom chose idiosyncratic, "crazy," meanings rather than none at all; but these idiosyncratic meanings placed him outside the framework of human consensus, thus escalating his confusion and making him more ill. This false meaning, incongruent with human consensus, ultimately deepened his suffering. The inability to make meaning in our lives ultimately leads to spiritual despair. The relationship between the duration of suffering and spiritual despair will become more clear as we proceed to a definition of suffering.

Spirituality and Suffering

When I approach the word *spiritual* I am aware of what Norman Cameron called "split level functioning."[12] Just as my private images of God range from the magical anthropomorphized images of childhood to the sweeping abstractions of a Teilhard de Chardin, so the meaning of the word *spiritual* functions at different levels in my being.[13] While the images of nonmaterial, super or extra-human beings such as ghosts or angels have faded beyond the developmental horizons of my life, they are not beyond recall. My childhood images of God seem to re-emerge as regressive responses to emotionally difficult moments. This is especially true of the hymns of my youth. Long forgotten, they reappear at the oddest times, cued to certain events in my life. At times I may find myself humming phrases from "Washed in the Blood" or "When We All Get to Heaven" even though my adult self feels that I have outgrown their simple theologies.

The writings of Ana-Maria Rizzuto have helped me to understand the origins of the more childish images of God and the more primitive conceptions of spirituality in my life.[14] The images of God, like the internal representations for important humans such as mother or father, are developed in specific periods of childhood. These tend to be reworked throughout successive stages of development allowing them to be integrated into the maturing personality. Even in mature personalities, however, early images lie buried in the psyche ready to be recovered under stressful circumstances. In more neurotic people the truncated maturational process has left such primitive images much nearer the surface.

As an adult I experience what I call spirituality in three primary ways: (1) as a sense of extrahuman presence, (2) as a sense of ultimate relatedness, and (3) as a sense of special significance for my life, as if I were being called to something beyond myself.

The sense of extrahuman presence is a common human experience. It is recognized in the writings of the mystics, and in the many spiritual visitations depicted in the Bible and throughout mythology and literature. These accounts range from apparitions and appearances to symbols, such as the tongues of fire at Pentecost, the pillar of fire in the desert, and the visitations of angels. In my own life this phenomenon has never assumed forms or shapes; it has been a quiet sense of numinous presence that was never far away.

I have been helped to understand the sense of ultimate relatedness, which I experience, by Tillich's theology of God as the ultimate ground of being.[15] I have been helped by Teilhard's writings to understand the sense of special significance (teleology) that calls me to higher levels of being.[16] All of these can be characterized in the Christian theological language that is central to my heritage. The sense of extrahuman presence becomes the Holy Spirit. The sense of being related to the ultimate becomes God the Ground of Being, and the sense of cosmic specialness becomes divinity incarnate in human existence.

I am convinced that these three qualities of "spirituality" exist for persons who do not share my own theological heritage. I have discussed these matters with Jewish colleagues who have stated that, while they have no sense of incarnation, they still share a feeling of ultimate relatedness and a sense of the specialness of their lives. As we proceed, I will attempt to make the point that it is at this deeper, more contextual, "spiritual" level that the meaning of life is interpreted. I will emphasize the thesis that when the events of life become too complex or too painful to be explained at this "spiritual" level, suffering occurs. This, I believe, lies at the core of suffering.

So, we have come upon several concepts that will prove critical to our understanding of suffering. Among them are such terms as *pain, external objects* and *inner images, self-consciousness, existential limits, meaning,* and *spirituality.* These are ideas to which we will return from time to time, as we form a definition of suffering.

The Human System and Suffering

If we view the human being as an interactive system with identity and self-consciousness, then we must begin to explore the relationships between the various parts of this system in order to further understand the causes and nature of suffering and the ways to alleviate it. Human existence is continually interpersonal, so we will explore suffering in the milieu of human relationships. And if we believe that all human activity is played out against the backdrop of some ultimate being, we must explore the spiritual elements of the sufferer's experience. Thus we have described at least three major interactive arenas that must be examined in order to understand suffering: the mind-body interaction, the sufferer's human relationships, and the sufferer's experience with the concept of Ultimate Being.

Others also have recognized the multiplicity of causes for suffering and have approached them from slightly different directions. Simone Weil noted three essential causes of suffering: physical, psychological, and social, all three of which are present in "true suffering."[17] Dorothee Soelle, while recognizing these same systems, added another dimension. She distinguished between "senseless suffering" (i.e., the social, political, and economic conditions that lead to hunger, oppression, and torture) and "potentially meaningful suffering," which enables a person to affirm the reality of

27

pain and to acknowledge suffering as an affirmation of life. In her thesis, even if one readily agrees that political oppression is senseless, one's response to it may still determine whether it is ultimately destructive or growth producing. One of Soelle's examples was the tortures of Auschwitz. In this objectively senseless situation, meaning can only be found in the individual human being's growth in integrity, dignity, and understanding, and certainly in the sufferer's relationship to God.[18]

In this discussion we are concerned with three major systems, the disruption of which can cause suffering for the individual human being. They are *the personal system:* the mind-body continuum and its interactive parts, *the interpersonal system:* the human being in his or her immediate social setting, and *the ontological system:* the human being in relation to Ultimate Being.

Eric Cassell presented similar ideas in an important article in the *New England Journal of Medicine:*

All the aspects of personhood—the lived past, the family's lived past, culture and society, roles, the instrumental dimension, associations and relationships, the body, the unconscious mind, the political being, the secret life, the perceived future, and the transcendent dimension—are susceptible to damage and loss. . . . If the injury is sufficient, the person suffers. The only way to learn what damage is sufficient to cause suffering, or whether suffering is present, is to ask the sufferer.[19]

Cassell managed to bring what threatened to be a smorgasbord of possibilities into a clear and constructive piece of writing. In his search for an understanding of suffering, he began, quite properly, with the statements of the sufferer.

For our purposes, let us assume that suffering is a multi-faceted phenomenon which can arise within the mind-body, interpersonal, or spiritual systems. These systems include physical, psychological, social, and spiritual dimensions. We recognize that changes in one dimension of a person's experience (i.e., physical, social, spiritual, etc.) are coincident with changes in other dimensions in a dynamic, interactive manner. But my thesis is that existential and spiritual issues lie at the heart of suffering.

We have attempted to establish the proposition that human beings are meaning-making and meaning-dependent for sanity, unity, and hope. Therefore, the disruption of meaning creates the confusion and despair that lie at the heart of suffering. Since meaning in any life crisis bears an important relationship to the person's sense of Ultimate Meaning, despair is finally a "religious illness" or a "pathology of faith."

Duration and Despair in Suffering

The word *suffer* comes to us through French from the two Latin words "sub" meaning "up," and "ferre" meaning "to bear:" to bear up. Webster's lists as the first meaning, "to submit to or be forced to endure." Other supporting meanings are, "to put up with, especially as inevitable or unavoidable; to endure death, pain, or distress; to sustain loss or damage; to be subject to disability or handicap."[20]

These definitions of suffering emphasize duration rather than intensity. Suffering means bearing up, enduring, putting up with, sustaining, or being subject to. This meaning is close to such idiomatic phrases as "long suffering" and "enduring patience." It implies that periods of intense pain are but incidents in the midst of suffering. Suffering itself is a state rather than an incident. It is not defined by sharp pains and moments of terror but by almost unbearable duration and inescapability. While this can be seen clearly in the description of Tom and by the statement from Job, it can also be seen in more common and ubiquitous situations. One need only go to the midway of a fair or carnival to see persons delightedly frightening themselves by riding monstrous inventions designed to provide *brief* periods of sheer terror. Thus, brief episodes of fear, undertaken in safety, are experienced as pleasure rather than suffering. Frightening oneself briefly and appropriately is common in children's play. It is called "active mastery" and is important to human development.[21]

But suppose a person discovered while riding the roller coaster that it could not be turned off. Pleasure would soon turn into fear, unbearable terror, and finally into intense suffering. Thus, pleasure and suffering may be separated by duration rather than by the intensity of the experience. As another example, how long would it take for the intensity of sexual gratification to turn into suffering if it could not be concluded?

It is interminability, rather than intensity, that is a key element in the experience of suffering. Short-term pain may lead to writhing, agony, and piteous crying out, but seemingly unending pain leads to resignation and despair. Experiments have shown that such resignation is evident even in lower animals. Maier's rats, when they could not solve the jumping stand problem (choosing the right-colored door to jump through when shocked), finally gave up the fight and sat hunched upon the jumping stand, resigned to the electric current.[22] They simply gave up hope and succumbed to misery.

A similar, human phenomenon has been observed in the torturing of prisoners of war. The prisoner's will is not broken by a single, or even by several episodes of torture, but by the sense that there is no hope. As we know from ministering to human beings who have surrendered to despair, death often lurks nearby. Such persons are often consumed by despairing ruminations, which become formalized into what Kovacs and Beck have called "depressive schemata."[23] These are mental structures that feature the "negative cognitive triad" consisting of negative thoughts about one's self, the world, and the future. These thoughts, once triggered, tend to run their course like repeated tape recordings. This repetitive quality makes it hard for caregivers to redirect the negative preoccupations of sufferers.

It is evident in both Tom's and Job's statements that an important ingredient in their expressions of suffering was the sense of despair, of interminability. However, despair need not be caused by such emotionally or physically traumatic events as these. Such ordinary human events as waiting, repetition, and boredom engender feelings of hopelessness and hence lie at the core of despair. Although Dante's concept of hell included physical pain, hopelessness was the ultimate metaphor for suffering as noted in the famous line "All hope abandon, ye who enter here" *(The Divine Comedy)*. Loss of hope is what has lain at the core of suffering for many of the depressed or physically handicapped persons I have tried to help.

We are aware that suicidal attempts are often not responses to short-term crises but efforts to terminate states of despair. It is when the pain of terror, loneliness, or physical illness seems interminable that death appears to be a welcome relief. Such feelings were eloquently expressed by Job during his nadir of hope:

> Let the day perish wherein I was born,
> and the night which said,
> "A man-child is conceived."
> Let that day be darkness!
> May God above not seek it,
> nor light shine upon it.
> (Job 3:3-4 RSV)

> Why did I not die at birth,
> come forth from the womb and expire?
> Why did the knees receive me?
> Or why the breasts, that I should suck?
> For then I should have lain down and been quiet;
> I should have slept; then I should have been at rest.
> (Job 3:11-13 RSV)

Enduring the unendurable is at the core of suffering, but what is unendurable may not be the same for each person. Boredom, hopelessness, physical pain, poverty, humiliation, or the phobic terrors of mental illness may be the "unendurable" for some; broken dreams, loneliness, and low self-esteem may be more central to the experience of suffering for others. Experiencing physical mutilation through trauma or accident is terrible, but living with the image-changing results can be much worse. The limited mobility and humiliation of an altered body image may be much harder to bear than the accident itself. Whatever causes despair, the loss of hope becomes the unendurable core of suffering. Fluctuations in hope and despair can affect the intensity of physical pain experienced by trauma sufferers. As we will discover in a later chapter, both the thresholds and the intensity of pain are related to such emotional variables as terror and despair.

Etched in my memory is the case of Mary, a lithe, charming woman who suffered a cardiac arrest during a rather routine operation. It left her with a number of ailments related to mobility and physical control. The most emotionally grinding of these problems was the need to wear a catheter because she could no longer control her urethral sphincter; for her, an intolerable humiliation. She knew she could no longer dance, but she would gladly have settled for the freedom to ride in a car without her damnable apparatus. It marred the self-concept of a once delicate, dainty, and beautiful woman. We struggled, through hours of psychotherapy together, attempting to help her gain perspective on her gloomy situation, with moderate success. She did, however, develop the energy to push for a new medical evaluation. I shall never forget the amazing transformation that took place in that woman when a newly devised operation was performed that restored muscular control. When that catheter was gone, all other pains and limitations became bearable. She became once more the cheerful and charming person she had always been. Although some physical pain and limitations in mobility remained, the suffering had largely ended. The pain and inconvenience caused by her handicapping problems were secondary to the intolerable blow to her self-esteem. The "real" suffering was caused by her diminished self-esteem and loss of hope.

Despair, the Ultimate Suffering

Kierkegaard, better than most writers, has made the point that physical suffering, even death, is not the ultimate suffering. It is not the physical indignities, the emotional confusion, or the social alienation that constitute the core of suffering, but the loss of hope: the despair. This is the real "sickness unto death." As he wrote in discussing the raising of Lazarus by Jesus:

> So then Lazarus is dead, and yet this sickness was not unto death. . . . But Christianly understood death is by no means the last thing of all, hence it is only a little event within that which is all, an eternal life; and Christianly understood there is in death infinitely much more hope than merely humanly speaking there is when there not only is life but this life exhibits the fullest health and vigor.
>
> Yet in another and still more definite sense despair is the sickness unto death. . . . the torment of despair is precisely this, not to be able to die. So it has much in common with the situation of the moribund when he lies and struggles with death, and cannot die.[24]

Kierkegaard has captured the epitome of suffering in this sad description of one who would rather be dead than to be locked in interminable despair. And he has also reinforced the concept introduced here earlier, that of all the ideas associated with suffering, despair or the failure of faith, as I have called it, is the most central.

Suffering and the Interactive Systems

In this chapter we have reviewed the systems in the human situation that are interactive in the experience of suffering: the physical, psychological, interpersonal, and spiritual. The physical aspects of suffering can have their points of origin either in the body itself or in social-emotional stresses that lead to physical symptoms. Writing on physical disability, Lee Meyerson proposed a continuum along which illnesses can be ranged to take into account the primacy of physical or psychological causes.[25] At one end of the continuum are psychosomatic illnesses, those emotionally caused physical problems that include peptic ulcers, colitis, and so on. Such illnesses are often directly responsive to environmental stressors. The other pole he called somatopsychic, referring to events based in physiology that either cause or are exacerbated by emotional concomitants. These include a range of illnesses from traumatic injuries to infectious and viral diseases such as cancer. So pain, which can act as a trigger for suffering, can arise either from within one's own body or from social and interpersonal stressors generating emotional reactions that are eventually harmful to the body.

An example of one of these directions is Tom, whose physical distress, real and imagined, was the result of tension and anxiety triggered by his faulty perceptions of the world around him. The case of Mary, the woman with the catheter, was an example of pain moving in the opposite direction. Her physical trauma occurred almost instantaneously, resulting in physically based pain, limited mobility, and a greatly damaged self-image. These two critical situations, beginning from different directions in the human interactive system, were both transformed into suffering by duration, creating confusion about the meaning and value of life, and leading to despair. It was not the point of origin, nor the pain itself that created the state of despair. It was the duration, confusion in meaning, and erosion of hope. Thus, what began as physical trauma on the one hand, and as social-emotional stress on the other, ended up in each case as a spiritual illness; a failure of hope resulting in despair and suffering.

Summary

In this chapter I tried to penetrate the experience of suffering with a series of questions touching on its physical, psychological, interpersonal, and spiritual aspects. This led to a discussion of the centrality of meaning in human experience, the roles of pain and duration in suffering, the importance of the concept of despair, and the conclusion that suffering arises when hope fails, and thus, is an essentially spiritual condition.

Suffering can be summarily defined, then, as a distressing state of human life arising from stress or tension in any part of the human interactive system—physical, psychological, interpersonal, or social and spiritual—and more related to the duration than to the intensity of emotional or physical pain. As stress continues over time it may cause confusion, loss of self-esteem, a sense of meaninglessness, and finally despair. The person involved may lose faith in himself or herself, God, the future, and positive human values. Deep cynicism, emotional withdrawal, or even suicide may result from the sufferer's attempt to escape from hopelessness.

However, suffering is neither inescapable nor irreversible. There may be three results from circumstances that "ought" to generate suffering. As we discovered from Bonhoeffer's writings, there are exceptional people who rise above suffering in situations where others despair.[26] Other persons sink into despair, only to discover new interpersonal, intellectual, and spiritual resources and recover. Still others, like Tom, are permanently damaged. We will try to understand why this is so.

The South African writer Alan Paton helps put our growing understanding of suffering into perspective:

All who are mature, whether young or old, accept suffering as inseparable from life; even if it is not experienced, the possibility of it is always there. I myself cannot conceive of life without suffering. There would certainly be no music, no theater, no literature, no art. I suspect that the alternative to a universe in which there is suffering, in which evil struggles with good and cruelty with mercy, would be a universe of nothingness, only an eternity of uninterrupted banality. If my suspicion is true, then I vote for the universe we have, where we have our joy that has been made real by suffering, as the silence of the night is made real by the sounds of the night. And we have our suffering there too, made real by our joy. Such a multifold universe, such a multifold life, despite all the unanswerable questions that they raise, seem more consonant with the idea of a creative and imaginative God than any garden of Eden.[27]

CHAPTER TWO

The Quality of Suffering

I have chosen to use the writings of Tolstoy to lead us more deeply into the experience of suffering. When he was about fifty years old Tolstoy passed through an excruciating period of melancholic suffering which he recounted in a book called *My Confession.*[1]

The Tale of the Traveler

In seeking a metaphor by which to explain this highly subjective experience to others, he came upon an old oriental fable about a traveler on the desert who was suddenly confronted by a wild beast. Terrified by the ferocious animal, the poor man jumped into a well. But as he was about to climb more deeply into the well he saw a dragon at the bottom with its mouth opened wide, ready to devour him. Not wishing to be eaten by the beast above or the beast below, the poor man clung to a wild bush growing out of one of the cracks in the well. While he clung there, with his hands weakening, he became aware that two mice, one white and one black, were moving evenly around the base of the bush, gnawing at its roots. While hanging between alternatives, waiting for fate to catch up to him, the traveler saw a few precious drops of honey glistening on the leaves of the bush where he clung. Tolstoy compared his own life to the traveler's dilemma:

The traveler sees this and knows that he must inevitably perish; but while thus hanging he looks about him and finds on the leaves of the bush some drops of honey. These he reaches with his tongue and licks them off with rapture.

Thus I hang upon the boughs of life, knowing that the inevitable dragon of death is waiting ready to tear me, and I cannot comprehend why I am thus made a martyr. I try to suck the honey which formerly consoled me; but the honey pleases me no longer, and day and night the white mouse and the black mouse gnaw the branch to which I cling. I can see but one thing: the inevitable dragon and the mice—I cannot turn my gaze away from them.

This is no fable, but the literal incontestable truth which every one may understand. What will be the outcome of what I do today? Of what I shall do tomorrow? What will be the outcome of my life? Why should I live? Why should I do anything? Is there in life any purpose which the inevitable death which awaits me does not undo and destroy?

Tolstoy had preceded the telling of this fable with the following graphic description of his situation:

Behold me then, a man happy and in good health, hiding the rope in order not to hang myself to the rafters of the room where every night I went to sleep alone; behold me no longer going shooting, lest I should yield to the too easy temptation of putting an end to myself with my gun.

I did not know what I wanted. I was afraid of life. I was driven to leave it; and in spite of that I still hoped something from it.

All of this took place at a time when so far as all my outer circumstance went, I ought to have been completely happy. I had a good wife who loved me and whom I loved; good children and a large property which was increasing with no pains taken on my part. I was more respected by my kinsfolk and acquaintances than I had ever been. I was loaded with praise by strangers; and without exaggeration I could believe my name already famous. Moreover I was neither insane nor ill.

Tolstoy was unable to account for the quality of his suffering within any "normal" conceptual framework. It seemed to be uniquely his, uniquely inexplicable, and uniquely terrifying. He was unable to find the cause of his suffering either within himself or within his circumstances. Yet he was able to communicate the power and poignancy of his suffering through a metaphor. As Don Browning has written: "None of us knows directly the ultimate context of experience; therefore we take more familiar and tangible aspects of experience and apply them metaphorically to the intangible and mysterious ultimate features of experience."[2]

Tolstoy's personal account of his own suffering and the fable metaphor he used to make it more universal, provide a doorway through which we may enter to understand the quality of suffering. It may help us understand what sufferers have in common, and why suffering takes different forms for different persons. We may come to see whether some of these forms are "normative" for certain personalities, and we may come to see that certain approaches to caring are more effective than others for certain "types" of sufferers. This seems an ambitious but necessary direction if we are to understand suffering more completely.

The Fable

In the fable, as in real life, the crisis precedes the dilemma. Having jumped into the well, one must choose whether to risk the danger above, the danger below, or to just hang on. How similar this is to the dilemma of the person who discovers he or she has advanced cancer. Should that person suffer the disease with as much dignity as possible until it ends life, or undergo a series of medical procedures with the remote possibility of a cure? And what of the person who finds herself in a brutal relationship? Should she risk breaking off the relationship with the possibility of disastrous financial consequences, even physical violence, or try to bear up under an intolerable situation? And should the person who finds himself in a shaky vocational situation in his middle years risk all accumulated security in order to take control of the situation, or hang on hoping that the branch will not break, dropping him into the jaws of the dragon of unemployment?

All of these too common possibilities are symbolized by the sense of sudden danger, of impending death so well described in the fable. As is the case with much suffering, the dilemma began with a crisis but soon settled into a continuing state of tension. This state was characterized by endless feelings of despair and helplessness. In order to bear it, the victim narrowed his perceptual focus, losing sight of the extended reality in which the drama took place. This greatly limited his ability to solve the problem. This too is a common response to suffering.

In the fable, only limited self-comforting behaviors were available, but even those began to fail. The honey of life was no longer sweet. There was a focus on the inevitability of death that crowded out potential joys and satisfactions. The comforts of a blue sky, a beautiful world, a life well filled with past blessings, memories of caring loved ones, remembered joys and successes, were lost from view as if they had never existed. The narrow focus on the dragon and the mice kept the poor victim from seeing the possibility of any creative solution of his problem. Creative solutions require an awareness of the context within which the dramas of life occur. Instead, an endless sense of loneliness, despair, and meaninglessness set in. There was no one to provide an Elijhan vision of fellow sufferers, to drive the wild beast away, or even to suggest that mice can be frightened rather easily. Thus, the poor traveler was caught in the condition essential to suffering: existential isolation, despair, and meaninglessness.

I have borrowed the term "existential isolation" from the writings of Yalom to express the particular quality of loneliness that lies at the core of suffering. The following quote defines his usage of the term:

Individuals are often isolated from others and from parts of themselves, but underlying these splits is an even more basic isolation that belongs to existence—an isolation that persists despite the most gratifying engagement with other individuals and despite consummate self-knowledge and integration. Existential isolation refers to an unbridgeable gulf between oneself and any other being. It refers, too, to an isolation even more fundamental—a separation between the individual and his world.[3]

To illustrate this point, Yalom quoted a patient as follows: "Remember the movie *West Side Story*, when the two lovers meet, and suddenly everything else in the world mystically fades away, and they are absolutely alone with one another? Well, that's what happens to me at these times. Except there's no one else there but me." This term not only fits Tolstoy's description of his own experience, but also suggests a kind of loneliness that, while it may be triggered by crises in relationships to others and ourselves, cannot be fully explained in that way. It is more understandable when cast in the framework of one's "ultimate context"; one's relationship to Ultimate Reality.

If we were to "break out" Tolstoy's metaphor for purposes of later discussion, it would go something like this: The wild animal is life with all its exhilarating, fearful challenges; the dragon is death; the well is the human predicament; the mice are the gnawing existential problems that beset us all, often leading to despair; and the honey is our ability to calm and soothe ourselves, to provide "holding introjects" that make terror and loneliness bearable.

Tolstoy opened up the discussion of suffering by describing his own experience and personified it by telling the story of his own confusion, despair, and suicidal thoughts. One wonders, with Tolstoy, how a man so successful could be so joyless; how a person with everything to live for could be contemplating suicide; how a person with an extended network of approving relationships could feel so alone. Yet, are these not the mice that gnaw at all our lives? Do we not all live with periods of self-doubt in the face of success, joylessness in the midst of beauty, and loneliness while in the bosom of our friends and families?

One might be tempted to write the whole thing off as an expression of Tolstoy's pathology, his melancholia. There are a number of depressive symptoms in his description of his situation. He seemed to have been obsessively concerned about his guns, to the point where he gave up hunting lest he harm himself. Such obsessions are often early symptoms of a major depressive episode. So is anhedonia: the inability to experience pleasure in response to usually pleasurable circumstances. So too is the narrowed perceptual focus that can only see negative contexts and consequences in life situations. These are the "depressogenic schemata," so predominant in the thinking of depressed persons.[4] It is as if a crisis in life has pushed the button on cognitive "tapes" that run off their depressive content once triggered. They are repeated to the exclusion of more positive facts and possibilities that are equally true of the person's situation. Like a penny held close to the eye, these obsessional negative thoughts obscure the whole world.

If Tolstoy were alive today, his potential major depression would likely be treated with medication that would increase the amount of serotonin in certain neurotransmitters of his brain, resulting in a marked reduction of the "depressive" symptoms. But what a great loss it would be if Tolstoy had been "cured" before he had the opportunity to open up the nature of his suffering for deeper consideration. Instead, he lived through it, broadening his search for meaning until he found a religious solution to his problem. He placed the problem where it existed, in an ontological context.

Despite the fact that some of his ideas were unusual, even bizarre, I accept Tolstoy's point that he was not suffering from a thought disorder. He stated plainly, "I was neither insane nor ill." His reality testing seemed unimpaired. He was a successful and prosperous man who found himself suffering from a more than ordinarily difficult midlife transition. He felt himself to be alone in the crowd without sufficient meaning around which to organize the "genera-tive" and "integrative" stages of his life.[5] For a period of time he hung helplessly in the well of his own "anomie."[6]

Like Tolstoy, many of us, not beset by overwhelming crises, live deeply alone inside a shell of achievement, vocational respect, and potentially loving interpersonal relationships. There, like Tolstoy, we die a little more every day. For us, the silent suffering seems interminable. The mice of our secret fears gnaw at the branch from which we cling. We may be caught, like Tolstoy, in the endless predicament of trying to understand why we suffer when things should be so good for us. For us, Santayana's words ring true:

Poets and philosophers sometimes talk as if life were an entertainment, a feast of ordered sensations; but the poets, if not the philosophers, know too well in their hearts that life is no such thing: it is a predicament. We are caught in it; it is something compulsory, urgent, dangerous, and tempting. We are surrounded by enormous, mysterious, only half-friendly forces.[7]

Suffering does not always require a discernible situational crisis. It is as if latent suffering becomes exposed with the erosion of time. When the rush toward credentialing, achievement, procreation, and child-rearing is interrupted by loss or illness or by the natural plateaus of aging; when we are forced to account for the value of our lives as we have lived them, the latent shadow of suffering hovers near our door. It is these realities revealed in Tolstoy's open sharing that are more important than questions of wellness or pathology. As Tolstoy himself has said, one need not be "sick" to suffer.

The reasons for suffering seem clearer when we can point to serious physical illness, handicapping conditions, or traumatic loss of loved ones, income, or status. But even when the precipitating conditions are clear, they do not account for the different responses of persons to the same crises. Some persons suffer while others do not, and some persons suffer much more intensely than others.

Tolstoy's story tells us that suffering cannot be understood solely by examining the economic circumstances, the physical condition, or even the human relationships of the sufferer. Neither the nature nor the intensity of suffering can be predicted from such conditions. We must look elsewhere to understand the causes, nature, and intensity of suffering. There must be prevenient causes within the sufferer, or within the environment in which she or he lives that are the predictors of the forms and levels of intensity that suffering will take.

Four Critical Structures

I believe that there are four *prevenient conditions* that have most to do with a person's vulnerability to suffering, and the manner in which he or she will respond to it. By calling them "prevenient," I mean that they precede or anticipate the experience of suffering.

By "conditions" I do not mean situations or circumstances, but conditions of. And in this context I mean the conditions of four different but related "structures." I believe it is the relative maturity, congruence, and completeness of these four structures that will determine the potential sufferer's resilience and integrity through the crises of suffering. I have labeled them the self-esteem structure, the self-protective structure, the ultimate context structure, and the human support structure.

Since the preferred definition of the word *structure* refers to the way something is built or organized rather than the product or substance itself, I believe the term is appropriate. These four structures are not topographical descriptions of "territories" within the person's life space in the manner of Freud's use of the terms *id* or *ego* in "The Anatomy of the Personality."[8] Perhaps Sullivan's term "dynamism" comes closer to what I mean by these structures, especially since they are not meant to be solely intrapsychic.[9] They are structures that include perceptions, cognitive arrangements, affects, and relationships around which portions of our human experience are organized. They are dynamic rather than status configurations, serving as frames of reference for our understanding of ourselves and our interactive experiences. Finally, such terms as *psychodynamic, interpersonal, intrapersonal, cognitive, developmental,* and *existential* may all be applied to one or more of these structures at any given time, but such words also fail to sufficiently convey the meaning I shall attempt to describe.

1. THE SELF-ESTEEM STRUCTURE

One critical variable in any person's ability to tolerate suffering is his or her level of self-esteem. As understandings of personality development have become influenced by Object Relations theorists, the term has become increasingly more important. The *self* has succeeded the *ego* as the most

43

important structure of the personality as modern theorists have shifted from a more Freudian to a more Object Relations perspective. One's own sense of having a good self, or more properly, of being a good self, is known as self-esteem. Ernest Becker, in his arresting style, has described the child's need for self-esteem as follows:

> In childhood we see the struggle for self-esteem at its least disguised. The child is unashamed about what he needs and wants most. His whole organism shouts the claims of his natural narcissism. And this claim can make childhood hellish for the adults concerned, especially when there are several children competing at once for the prerogatives of limitless self-extension, what we might call "cosmic significance." The term is not meant to be taken lightly, . . . it expresses the heart of the creature: the desire to stand out, to be *the* one in creation. When you combine natural narcissism with the basic need for self-esteem, you create a creature who has to feel himself an object of primary value: first in the universe, representing in himself all of life. . . . An animal who gets his feeling of worth symbolically has to minutely compare himself to those around him, to make sure he doesn't come off second-best. . . . he must desperately justify himself as an object of primary value in the universe; he must stand out, be a hero, make the biggest possible contribution to world life, show that he counts more than anything or anyone else.[10]

This presentation of the human need for self-esteem is loaded with masculine psychological assumptions and language. Perhaps that is why it resonates so powerfully with my own childhood experience. Yet it gets at the heart of a central human theme that may be equally true for both men and women, that is, the need for a sense of "cosmic specialness." Carol Gilligan's writings suggest that girls may more often experience a sense of being special through relationship and joining, rather than through competition.[11] But whether it is fulfilled through relationship or competition, the need to be the most important, the most loved, the most special may reign supreme during a period of normal narcissistic grandiosity. The recognition of the human need for specialness runs through the writings of the Neo-Freudians, Object Relations theorists, and feminist psychologists. It also has a rather sound theological basis, if one considers the biblical writings, which see humans as being a "little lower than the angels," and "made in the image and likeness of God" (Ps. 8:5; Gen. 1:26-27).

Although this need for cosmic specialness may not be expressed so blatantly during adulthood, it is not dead; it has simply gone underground. A whole range of closed social groups, ranging from religious cults to private clubs, appeal to the human need to be more special than others. Credit cards are sold by the millions through an appeal to this need. One of the developmental qualities that may be most under attack during periods of suffering is this sense of cosmic specialness that lies at the core of one's personal sense of meaning. Midlife crises often occur when we discover that we are not, and may never be, as special as we needed to be.

Self-Esteem and Childhood Development

Modern Object Relations theorists have moved away from Freud's drive-oriented libido theory in their attempts to understand the importance of self-esteem. They have focused more on the importance of parenting figures as "self-objects."[12] Infants initially feel psychologically conjoint with these parenting figures, receiving psychological nurture as if the two of them were one being. As a more independent self-structure is developed, children must still look to these modeling and supporting others to help them maintain integrity and well-being.

Heinz Kohut and Ernest Wolfe, in their article on disorders of the self, have provided a succinct summary of the manner in which the self develops.

It is in the matrix of a particular selfobject environment that, via a specific process of psychological structure formation called *transmuting internalization,* the *nuclear self* of the child will crystallize. . . . We can say 1) that it cannot occur without a previous state in which the child's mirroring and idealizing needs had been sufficiently responded to; 2) that it takes place in consequence of the minor, non-traumatic failures in the responses of the mirroring and the idealized selfobjects; and 3) that these failures lead to the gradual replacement of the selfobjects and their functions by a self

45

and its functions. . . . The ultimate wholesome result, the autonomous self, is not a replica of the selfobject.[13]

As the separation of the child from these selfobjects proceeds during maturation, several important changes take place that have enormous implications for the person's ability to handle future crises and losses. One of the most important of these is the development of self-esteem. The child must learn to interpret and internalize expressions of regard, affection, approval, and disapproval of the self. Sullivan called these "reflected appraisals."[14] Positive reflected appraisals become transformed into what Dan Buie and Gerald Adler, in their analysis of borderline personalities, have called "holding introjects," with which one may soothe oneself during periods of temporary separation from selfobjects.[15] These reflected appraisals consist not only of statements of approval and prohibition but also of attitudes, gestures, and general body language on the part of mothering and fathering selfobjects, which Sullivan called "significant others." Some of these positive appraisals can be remembered throughout a lifetime, but more often they are lost as building blocks in permanently positive feelings about oneself.

Self-Esteem and Aloneness

Among the most important changes that take place during this maturational process is a growing awareness that the self and the selfobjects are not unitary. In most Object Relations theories, the anxiety that provides the underlying motivation for the development of self is not a result of libidinal drives but the result of feelings of intolerable aloneness without the selfobject. Even when a child views the self as "good" and is able to develop an integrated view of his or her person, aloneness is still intolerable without frequent stroking. This stroking comes in the forms of positive verbal cues, smiles, and actual physical holding and stroking. Modern psycho-physiologists are learning through experimentation that humans are actually neuronically "wired" for such stroking.

Such research follows up early observations made by René Spitz and others of infants separated from their parents during the Second World War.[16] Such children, though provided with adequate sustenance and cleanliness, showed signs of agonizing grief and loneliness. They were both emotionally and physiologically underdeveloped, often showing signs of severe pathology. The proofs are accumulating that what we instinctively know to be true is scientifically true: Love is essential for human survival.

As the child matures, cognition and memory permit that child to transform these positive experiences into holding introjects, which may be used for self-soothing during periods of aloneness. As we grow older all of us have a repertoire of memories that can be invoked when enforced loneliness causes a rise in separation anxiety. I can still remember how essential to my well-being were the vivid images of my wife and two young children when I was stranded for a few days on an isolated lake in Northern Ontario because the cloud ceiling was too low for the float plane to take off or land. The sense that someone loves us, or that we love ourselves, or that we are lovable, is a critical deterrent to low self-esteem, and hence to suffering.

Self-Esteem and Healthy Narcissism

In modern child-rearing, we have learned not to worry so much about "spoiling" children. Narcissism has been accepted as a normal developmental phase in the lives of human beings. We have learned that the child becomes strong through acceptance, approval, and interaction. Only then can the process of individuation begin. This helps the child develop holding introjects that provide a self-soothing, comforting, positive self-regard during those increasingly long periods of time when stroking from significant others is not available. Holding introjects consist of images, feelings memories, and other reassurances that have been "filed" away for future use. Such holding introjects often include images of God.[17] As the child grows emotionally and intellectually, these holding introjects must expand to cosmic dimensions if he or she is to manage cosmic events such as death and personal catastrophes with reasonable comfort.

Almost every little child knows the delightful sense of forgiveness that occurs after an angry narcissistic outburst, when the "bad me" has disrupted trust between the child and the "mothering one." The child is gathered into the parent's arms and held with cooing physiological acceptance. Nothing is so safe or good. If we are to be safe from our self-blame and self-hatred during periods of suffering, it is important for our horizons to have enlarged enough to include a safe and orderly universe and the sense of an ultimate parenting figure who cares what happens to us.

In simple terms, it is important for the child in us to feel that he or she is lovable, that the world is an essentially good and safe place, and that periods of loneliness are not permanent but will end in reunion with significant others. These are essential preconditions if the self is to retain its integrity during periods of suffering.

Self-Esteem and Anxiety

It is our self-esteem consisting of internalized appraisals, growing physiological competencies, a sense of self-sufficiency, and the freedom to initiate action without undue separation anxiety, that allows us to survive. The immobilizing enemy is anxiety. Too much anxiety will not only result in permanently low self-esteem, but may also retard development, leaving the person uncertain, confused, and dependent. Deficiencies in the development of self-esteem leave the person particularly vulnerable during periods of loneliness, separation, loss, and physical illness. During such periods there is a greater possibility for fragmentation of the self, with various potential forms of pathology. Attempts to cope may result in perceptually narrowed, obsessional suffering with a loss in the ability to maintain interpersonal support systems. The culmination of this negative process is existential isolation.

Conclusions

I believe that there are two conclusions, drawn from the Object Relations literature, that are particularly helpful in our understanding of suffering. The first is that suffering is an experience that increases loneliness. The normal precipitants to suffering are personal physical changes such as sickness or injury, loss of income, status or vocational identity, loss of loved ones, or loss of relational meaning as a result of aging. All of these conditions tend to increase the sense of existential isolation. Feeling alone and powerless over a long period of time can lead to feelings of despair. These may be so intense that a person will "give up" efforts to remain in vital contact with other people and events. Suffering then becomes a series of self-fulfilling prophecies. "No one cares about me," "No one understands me," "My life doesn't matter to anyone," "I might as well be dead."

The second conclusion is that loneliness will place great pressure on one's self-esteem structure. Normal sources of acceptance, assurance, and stroking may not be available. External sources for the reinforcement of self-esteem may be greatly diminished. The longer suffering lasts and the less hope there is for permanent recovery from illness, or the replacement of losses, the more one is threatened by despair. Two major dangers lurk when aloneness turns to despair for persons with marginal self-esteem structures. The first is the fragmentation of the self, with attendant psychopathology, and the second is the development of suicidal thoughts.

When tragedies come into our lives we are called on to use the integrity of our self-systems as never before. Somehow we must continue to function. Often it is in carrying out the mundane details of our daily lives that we are able to shift the focus away from potential disaster to the richness of daily life. We may be called on to create our own "holding introjects" during periods of pain and isolation. During such times a sense of "cosmic specialness" is particularly important. Images of a loving and sustaining God are particularly useful as holding introjects. It is also helpful to have a repository of positive interpersonal memories to reinforce our sense of personal worth, especially when it is impossible by reason of age or illness to "prove" our value to ourselves. All of these tactics serve to strengthen self-esteem, helping us to feel less powerless and alone during periods of suffering.

2. THE SELF-PROTECTIVE STRUCTURE

As human beings, we find it hard to let ourselves know everything that we are, and we can never let others know. This point is made by most major personality theorists. Freud used the idea of the repressed unconscious to indicate that much of our own experience is unknown to us; that is unknown to our "self." Such writers as Sullivan and Rogers have pointed out that much of our experience is unsymbolized as being part of our selves.[18] It is part of neither the "good me" nor the "bad me," but remains in the "not me" category. Object Relations theorists see the child as omitting unapproved behavior from the self-structure. And in cases where selfobjects fluctuate unpredictably in their responses of approval and disapproval, a "split" may develop wherein the child fluctuates between intense feelings of good me and bad me as if they belonged to separate selves.

The more fully one knows one's own experience, accepts it as part of oneself, and integrates it into one's self-concept, the greater one's personal power is in the face of crisis. One of the goals of traditional psychotherapy has been to acquaint the self with the unknown, often feared, parts of one's own being. Getting acquainted with one's feared impulses in a setting of safety is the psychotherapeutic substitute for having loving parents and siblings to support the child in learning to expose and control feelings of anger, rivalry, and fear. For the person who has matured in one of these ways, through either a "safe" childhood or psychotherapy, the unconscious holds fewer surprises; the power of impulses is known and the less desirable side of oneself is recognized, becoming available for transformation.

THE QUALITY OF SUFFERING

The Risk of Being Godlike

Even in the best of circumstances we seem unable to bear all of our own experience. When I say "unable to bear" I mean that we are overwhelmed by anxiety if we know too much about ourselves. On the one hand we fear being overwhelmed by our own power; not simply by our sexual or hostile impulses as Freud would have had us think, but by our own creative and procreative powers as well. We dare not compete with the gods. This situation seems to me to have two equally important points of reference; one of these is the selfobjects on whom we have been so dependent. Our experience teaches us to fear that if we are strong we will lose them forever. Too often parents challenge our expanding narcissism with questions like, "Who do you think you are?" or authority statements like, "I'm in charge of this house, not you!" We soon learn that there is an implicit risk in not being dependent and deferential enough. We dare not fully learn about our anger, or our parents' moments of weakness and undependability; for to lose parental support is symbolically to die. Unfortunately, children often project these limited, authoritarian qualities onto their images of God as well.

But it is also risky to be too godlike in a more cosmic sense. We cannot bear to know our badness, sinfulness, or vulnerability because it is such a powerful reminder of our thinly masked mortality. If we live too fully we may die, if we admit our vulnerability and imperfection, our sinfulness, we may die. So we may die from too much power as well as from too much weakness. Becker has captured these ideas with unique clarity:

So one of the first things a child has to do is to learn to "abandon ecstasy," to do without awe, to leave fear and trembling behind. Only then can he act with a certain oblivious self-confidence, when he has naturalized his world. We say "naturalized" but we mean unnaturalized, falsified, with the truth obscured, the despair of the human condition hidden, a despair that the child glimpses in his night terrors and daytime phobias and neuroses. This despair he avoids by building defenses; and these defenses allow him to feel the basic sense of self-worth, of meaningfulness, of power. They allow

51

him to feel that he controls his life and his death, that he really does live and act as a willful and free individual, that he has a unique and self-fashioned identity, that he is *somebody*—not just a trembling accident germinated on a hothouse planet. . . . We called one's life style a vital lie, and now we can understand better why we said it was vital: it is a *necessary* and basic dishonesty about oneself and one's whole situation.[19]

Becker proposes that all of us must build an explanatory, defensive system that is an apologia for our lives. We build a depersonalizing descriptive facade that speaks of ourselves in terms of achievements, possessions, college degrees, vocational expertise, religious or moral probity, and so on. It has little to do with who we are inside. It does not speak of our dreams, loves, vulnerabilities, aspirations, and longings. Nor does it include those times when we neglect our own principles, a neglect that contradicts the facade that takes the place of genuine self-esteem.

I remember having the most uncomfortable time with the word "happy." People insisted on asking me if I was happy: "Are you happy with your new job?" "Are you happy living in Boston?" "Are you happy with your house?" "Are you happy?" This question was awkward at that time for several reasons. First, because I never thought about work or possessions in terms of happiness. Goodness, love, self-respect, acceptance—these were the kind of words that seemed more related to happiness. Besides, who had a right to be happy? It might indeed be safer to speak of one's work as "interesting" or "challenging," one's house as a "good buy," one's children as "well behaved." To look deeply into the question, Am I happy? might explode the carefully constructed apologia for one's life. As Becker would have it, one's "vital lie."

Suffering Explodes the Vital Lie

Suffering has a tendency to explode the vital lies of our lives. We cannot escape careful review of the quality of our lives. Reinforcement of the vital lie is interrupted during periods of suffering. Bricks fall from the defensive wall and we may find that many of the things that absorbed our energy are utterly useless when suffering comes to call. If Becker is correct in implying that life in its totality is too much for any of us, that we must erect a vital lie just as God threw up a hand at the mouth of a cave to protect Moses' eyes from the full glory of the world, then we may be in trouble when suffering interrupts the game of life. We suffer, in part, because we are forced to unmask the lies *as* lies and to catch a glimpse of the "ecstacy" we have "abandoned." As we will discover later, there is little suffering that does not carry remorse on its back.

The more realistic our own evaluation of our strengths and weaknesses, the quality of our support relationships, and the nature of the world around us, the better things will turn out to be when suffering strikes. If we don't "lie" too much to ourselves we will have a more balanced view of what we might call reality. But reality and pessimism are not equivalent words. Pessimism may protect us from false expectations, but it will also keep us from growing, and perhaps most important, from hoping.

3. The Ultimate Context Structure

If we are to solve any one of life's problems, it is important to consider the frame within which the problem exists. A mildly upset stomach does not require surgery or laying on of hands; normally, a small dose of bicarbonate will do. Stress created by loss of a job can most often be handled with the support of family and friends, good vocational counseling, and recourse to a job placement agency. A case of chronic dysthymia can normally be treated by using moderate medication and a good deal of psychotherapy. Every problem is not a life-threatening tragedy, but it is important to recognize such a tragedy when we see it and to realize that its understanding requires a much larger frame of reference. The frame within which all problems are considered must be expanded as the problem becomes more complex and includes more of the systems that make up the socio-psycho-physiological context within which human life is lived. Some of the difficulties with suffering are that even this tridimensional frame is not large enough and that the systems within the frame shift and interpenetrate. The results and causes of suffering are often interchangeable. For example, physical trauma may cause emotional suffering, which may further exacerbate the physical trauma. Suffering may engage us at every level of our existence. It is to be expected that physical, psychological, and interpersonal systems will always be involved in suffering, but I believe that the frame must be enlarged beyond these three systems if we are to understand suffering more completely.

Let us return to Tolstoy for a moment to see how he framed the "territory" of his suffering. This rather lengthy passage begins with the existential questions we quoted earlier and continues:

Why should I live? Why should I do anything? Is there in life any purpose which the inevitable death which awaits me does not undo and destroy?

These questions are the simplest in the world. From the stupid child to the wisest old man, they are in the soul of every human being. Without an answer to them, it is impossible, as I experienced, for life to go on. . . .

And I sought for an explanation in all the branches of knowledge acquired by men. I questioned painfully and protractedly and with no idle curiosity. I sought, not with indolence, but laboriously and obstinately for days and nights together. I sought like a man who is lost and seeks to save himself—and I found nothing. I became convinced, moreover, that all those who before me had sought for an answer in the sciences have also found nothing. And not only this, but they have recognized that the very thing which was leading me to despair—the meaningless absurdity of life—is the only incontestable knowledge accessible to man.[20]

Placing the Problem in the Ultimate Context

I deplore the modern tendency toward post facto analyses of historical figures, figures long gone from this world who cannot answer back. It sometimes amuses me that Freud, the first great psychoanalyst, seems to be the favorite post facto target of those using his own methods to analyze historical figures.

However, I do believe it is fair to say that Tolstoy was looking for the answer to his dilemma within the wrong frames of reference. He tried to find a scientific-philosophical answer to a problem that existed at other levels of his being. I remember the words of an old-time preacher spoken in my hearing many years ago: "You might as well try to feed a hungry horse by tearing a page out of the Bible and giving it to him to eat as to try to satisfy the soul with things."

It is not so difficult for an itch to be scratched or a hunger to be satisfied if one can locate the source of the discomfort. In attempting to do this, Tolstoy ran into what I call the "Vienna Circle Dilemma." He tried to measure complex human matters on a limited scientific scale. The data would have had to be distorted in order to provide any answer at all, and by then the question would have become irrelevant. But Tolstoy, realizing this, struggled to reframe the question of why life had lost its meaning. He did this by reanalyzing the data of his own experience, and in so doing he penetrated his own "vital lie":

Yet, whilst my intellect was working, something else in me was working too, and kept me from the deed [suicide]—a consciousness of life, as I may call it, which was like a force that obliged my mind to fix itself in another direction and draw me out of my situation of despair. . . . During the whole course of this year. . . . my heart kept languishing with another pining emotion. I call this by no other name than that of a thirst for God. This craving for God had nothing to do with the movement of my ideas—in fact, it was the direct contrary of that movement—but it came from my heart. It was like a feeling of dread that made me seem like an orphan and isolated in the midst of all these things that were so foreign. And this feeling of dread was mitigated by the hope of finding the assistance of some one.

Tolstoy reframed his dilemma as a spiritual problem. He appears to have come to see the problem, not as one requiring cognitive solutions, but as a problem in the relationship between himself and God. Tolstoy's naked sharing of his experience created a response in me that says the loss of meaning in life is most often a spiritual problem and our relationship with God is always the ultimate context.

Theologian David Roberts has made a comment relevant to this point in his discourse on Kierkegaard:

Man in despair usually regards himself as a victim of external circumstances, but when he recognizes that the trouble is internal, he only intensifies his predicament if he tries to cure himself. For it is only one whose proper destiny is fellowship with God who could fall into a disease which is intrinsically spiritual. . . . Unlike a physical illness, despair does not simply run its course once it is contracted; on the contrary, it is being contracted in every instant, for it is related to the eternal in man. Instead of literally killing a person it involves the torment of not being able to die. It manifests man's linkage to eternity in a negative way in that he can consume himself indefinitely without getting rid of the self.[21]

Differing Views of the Ultimate Context

Of course, everyone does not share this theological view of ultimate context, and there are great variations in images of God among persons whose sense of ultimate context does include an explicit belief in a supreme being. These images range from God as present and available (immanent) to God as distant and transcendent, and God as supra-humanly personal to God as an overarching organizing Principle. Many of us who have been trained in social science and theology find ourselves in a tug between Revelation and Research. I use capitals because each of these has become an idol in its respective theoretical context. On the one hand, we cannot have respect among our scientific colleagues unless we base our ideas on data and use an appropriate number of linguistic shibboleths that indicate respect for the demi-god research. On the other hand, if scientific research, or even the data experience, becomes a primary reference in our theorizing, questions about our faith may be raised among our more theological colleagues. We may be accused of idolatry because we have forgotten that faith is essential to an understanding of ultimate context and that faith comes only as a gift of God.

Several important writers in psychology have avoided this dilemma by recognizing the need for an "ultimate frame" without using any of the Judeo-Christian labels for God. They have recognized that "something ultimate" is going on in human growth without expressing this "spiritual" belief in theological language. Erich Fromm, in listing the qualities of normative "humanness," emphasized the need for rootedness and a sense of transcendence as being necessary to meaning and purpose in life.[22] To be truly human, a person must be rooted in his or her cultural experience and have a vision of the world that transcends place and culture. This transcendence appears to have a teleological quality that pulls us toward higher levels of wholeness without which we would remain animals.

In his study of especially creative persons, Abraham Maslow recognized the presence of a "transcendent" world view among such highly "self-actualizing" persons.[23] Carl Rogers also used the term *self-actualization,* providing a rather complete definition:

The directional trend we are endeavoring to describe is evident in the life of the individual organism from conception to maturity, at whatever level of organic complexity. It is also evident in the process of evolution, the direction being defined by a comparison of life low on the evolutionary scale with types of organisms which have developed later. . . .

Ideas similar to this proposition are being increasingly advanced and accepted by psychologists and others. The term "self-actualization" is used by Goldstein to describe this one basic striving. Mowrer and Kluckhohn stress the "basic propensity of living things to function in such a way as to preserve and increase integration."[24]

Rogers pointed out that a number of other theorists (e.g., Harry Stack Sullivan, Karen Horney) hold similar views, and he ended by quoting Angyal:

Life is an autonomous dynamic event which takes place between the organism and the environment. Life processes do not merely tend to preserve life but transcend the momentary status quo of the organism, expanding itself continually and imposing its autonomous determination upon an ever increasing realm of events.[25]

These ideas closely follow Teilhard de Chardin's conclusions drawn from his years of experimental study in biology.[26] His evolutionary thesis was that all species, including the human species, move toward more complete explication of their own natures and toward higher levels of consciousness. He unabashedly saw God as the teleological center of this activity. This, it seems to me, is a more complete and honest view of the observable evolutionary direction of both individuals and species. It does not stop with a nebular concept of some kind of "growth principle" but pictures nature as being "called" to higher experience. Although the question is moot whether this occurs through some kind of genetic imprint or through a teleological pull, Teilhard names the source as God.

Implicit in the beliefs of these writers is that human life has an orderly, intentional frame; and that in all creatures there is movement toward higher development and consciousness. This central thrust toward maturity enhances the meaning of life. To believe this helps give persons the courage to move forward in the face of adversity.

Being Honest About the Ultimate Context

In reviewing this section of the manuscript a trusted colleague wrote, "Your own fundamental assumption of self-actualization *illustrates* your 'ultimate context' but is not necessarily normative. Considering how central it is to your own thinking, might it be located *outside* of what I call your four 'diagnostic' categories?"

What strikes me in response to this reasonable comment is the many times I have had discussions with scholars who behaved as if there were an ultimate context that had an effect on the direction of human life, but who expressed these views in humanistic terms. Their views came out as demythologized theological assumptions lacking in power. It was as if these ideas were truncated short of their logical objective. I prefer to be open about this basic underlying assumption in my own thinking.

Ultimate Context as a Framework for Healing

It is especially helpful to the sufferer to be able to place his or her individual struggles in an *extended temporal context:* "This too shall pass away"; *an extended interpersonal context:* "Many others have lived through these sorrows before me"; and *an extended spiritual context:* "There is Someone beyond all this who knows and cares that I suffer."

One of the great mysteries of the therapeutic process, for me, has been the courage of clients moving forward in the face of anxiety, to resolve the very problems that frightened them most. Even though increased awareness of themselves threatened the vital lie that they had so carefully constructed to keep themselves from knowing the worst about themselves, they were willing to suffer in order to become more whole. Does this happen because a unique DNA message written in their biological structure pushes them toward growth, or because the Spirit of God beckons them to become more than they are? Is one of these views less viable than the other? Would not either conclusion require the idea of a transcendent intelligence as its causal base?

Attitude and Healing

Most caregivers are aware that a special ingredient exists in healing that has to do with attitude, the willingness to suffer in order to grow. Rogers underscored my experience as both minister and psychotherapist with the following words.

It is our experience in therapy which has brought us to the point of giving this proposition a central place. The therapist becomes very much aware that the forward-moving tendency of the human organism is the basis upon which he relies most deeply and fundamentally. It is evident not only in the general tendency of clients to move in the direction of growth when the factors in the situation are clear, but is most dramatically shown in very serious cases where the individual is on the brink of psychosis or suicide.

Here the therapist is very keenly aware that the only force upon which he can basically rely is the organic tendency toward ongoing growth and enhancement.[27]

God as Ultimate Context

Tolstoy, the sufferer, did not speak about an "organic tendency" toward enhancement. He spoke about a thirst for God. He felt like "an orphan and isolated in the midst of all these things that were so foreign."[28]

Sensing a return of the engulfing, fragmenting loneliness of the undeveloped self, he longed for a cosmic "selfobject" to whom he might join himself. It is helpful in times of great crisis to have a world view that includes a sense of positive direction, orderliness, and a loving Intelligence to whom we may turn. Rogers' "organic tendency" and Tolstoy's "thirst" appear to be, respectively, more objective and more subjective descriptions of the same growth-seeking phenomenon.

When Tolstoy recognized his lost sense of meaning and subsequent despair as a religious problem, he began to get well. Consider his post-traumatic paean in praise of faith:

Since mankind has existed, wherever life has been, there also has been the faith that gave the possibility of living. Faith is the sense of life, that sense by virtue of which man does not destroy himself, but continues to live on. It is the force whereby we live. . . . The idea of an infinite God, of the divinity of the soul, of the union of men's actions with God—these are ideas elaborated in the infinite secret depths of human thought. They are ideas without which there would be no life, without which I myself would not exist. I began to see that I had no right to rely on my individual reasoning and neglect these answers given by faith, for they are the only answers to the question.

So Tolstoy solved his problem in what Barth would have called a "providential" manner. Geoffrey Bromiley has distilled Barth's view of belief in providence. "First it is faith in the strict sense, not an idea, postulate, conclusion, or value-judgement, but faith in God, not in the creature, a cosmic process, or a system. Hence it must not be equated with a philosophy of history, which may or may not be useful."[29]

This certainly seems congruent with the experience of Tolstoy. He looked for a solution in science and in philosophical systems without success. He needed a frame of reference that was both more cosmically special and very personal. His frame of reference became more ultimate, in that he turned to God as the Ground of Being, and more personal in that he reached out to an Ultimate Person through faith.[30] Thus, in one resolving moment he arrived at a solution that led him out of confusion and to a personal relationship, which penetrated his profound aloneness. This is what religious faith has often done for believers.

Barth, as have many other theologians, placed limits on faith that make it difficult for a social scientist to embrace. To quote from Bromiley's view of Barth's position: "Finally, belief in providence is faith in Christ. It knows God, not as a general God of providence, but as the God of fatherly providence, the Father of Jesus Christ. It parts company here not only with pantheism and polytheism but also with Judaism."[31]

At this point Bromiley quoted Barth directly: "The Christian belief in providence is Christian and . . . must not be . . . an extract from what Jews, Turks, pagans and Christians may believe in concert."[32]

It may be just such christological insistence that has caused writers such as Rogers, Fromm, Maslow, and others to develop frames for the explanation of the human drive toward wholeness that fell short of any recognition of God as the ultimate cause for such a growth principle. Or it may account in part for the propensity of pastoral counselors, who are at least moderately theologically educated, to use more existential theological approaches such as Tillich's God as Ground of Being. This idea seems to leave the concept of God less christologically personal but more congruent with scientific points of view.

When the Ultimate Context Is Known and Shared

It is a common experience to see the importance of faith in the healing process. The combination of skill and faith that

61

the practitioner brings to the suffering one, and the sufferer's belief about his or her ability to get well, are crucial ingredients of the healing process. A sense of positive providential support is often shared between caregiver and the recipient of care. I have been impressed with the fact that "God's work," the work of healing, is done well by those who believe in this providential compact, regardless of the manner in which they frame their beliefs.

Although it is most important that there be a frame of ultimate context, it need not be identical for the sufferer and caregiver. But if the caregiver does not understand and respect the framing beliefs of the sufferer, the work of healing is clearly impeded. In the case of psychotherapy, it is important for the therapist to develop a picture of the client's frame of reference that includes developmental history, important metaphors (these may be in the form of "key incidents" or "special memories"), and linguistic conventions. This allows responses to be framed so that they are palatable and congruent with the client's self system.

I shall never forget an incident that occurred when, as a local pastor, I visited an elderly gentleman. He was a still distinguished ex–bank president who had had a series of strokes and heart attacks that left him with residual unilateral paralysis and some aphasia. It was my custom to visit him at least every other week at the nursing home where I found him in his wheelchair. However, when I visited him after a fairly long vacation in Mexico, he greeted me as follows: "You've been here seldom lately!" I said, "Yes, that's true; it's been several weeks. What shall I do about it?" He said, "You can apologize and come more often." I had mistaken his "frame." He was more aware of my visits than I, or the nurses around him, would have thought possible. I also learned that the relationship was more important to his sense of well-being than I had realized; his expectations of my caring were not casual and he mustered all the language at his command to make me aware of this. This man, damaged by a series of heart attacks and cerebro-vascular accidents, with his aphasic limitations, had retained a metaphor that was central to his ultimate context. The minister represented the presence of God. I had forgotten the metaphor, but he had not.

When the Ultimate Context Is Negative

I am arrested by a distressing thought in concluding this section. I have framed a positive view of the Ultimate Context which, if used by the sufferer and those who provide care, will enhance the process of recovery. Even when recovery from physical illness is not possible, recovery of faith, courage, and human relationships may occur in the process of dying. (This idea is explicated convincingly by Mwalimu Imara in *Death: The Final Stage of Growth*.)[33]

But what happens if sufferers do not have such a world view? Suppose they experience the world as a negative, punitive place or believe that their present state of suffering is the result of their own sins? Some may view God as a punitive, authoritarian figure who is out to get them. It is at this point that the human support system becomes most important. The persons who surround the sufferer quietly become the conveyors of the grace of acceptance; they become vehicles for the sufferer's self-forgiveness.

4. THE HUMAN SUPPORT STRUCTURE

The quality of persons the sufferer is able to gather around himself or herself may be more crucial to healing than any of the technologies (medical, psychological, pastoral) that are available. The placebo effect created by an aura of understanding and acceptance, a genuine valuing of the sufferer, may be instrumental in extending the sufferer's world view to include faith in a loving ultimate context. The positive views of caregivers cannot be overestimated as aids to healing.

The caregiver's positive world view must not be faked, or used as a kind of psychological injection. Nothing is more superficial than professional positivism that skims across the surface of the sufferer's pain without ever touching anything that matters. This is often particularly inappropriate in the treatment of the elderly. All of us have heard caregivers stripping away the dignity from suffering persons by ignoring their shame and humiliation in the face of helplessness. Sometimes insult is added to injury by the use of disparaging language. I cringed when I heard the afore-mentioned ex–bank president addressed, "Come on George, be a good boy and take your medicine. Let's move you to your wheelchair while I make your bed and you can have a nice nap."

Sufferers do need cleanliness, structure, and limits, but more than that they need understanding. Often they do not want cheap grace in the form of distant, easy acceptance. They may need the opportunity to confess. They may need to tell the story of how they feel they have failed themselves and others. They may need for us to know how serious this all seems to be to them. When sufferers are treated seriously, as persons of intrinsic worth, healing can take place.

I remember visiting a distinguished executive, who was afflicted with both cancer and brain deterioration and was being treated as a lover by his wife of more than fifty years. All through the months of his deteriorating illness, she never forgot who he was. There was no baby talk, no misunder-standing of his unpredictability, forgetfulness, and occasion-al irascibility. She had a clear image of his irreplaceable value and addressed him with respect and tender affection at the most difficult of times.

Religious rituals, such as prayer or the eucharist, are redemptive metaphors that often exist within the ultimate context of the sufferer. These symbols may hold when illness has affected judgment and rationality. As Tolstoy pointed out, our salvation does not depend on our ability to "figure things out." Tolstoy, a consummate intellectual, began to heal when he yielded to historical theological wisdom, corporate worship, and the call of his own faith. These worked for him when logical proofs and explanations failed. It is in this area that the clergyperson is a valuable member of the human support team.

Many sufferers feel that they have sinned and need forgiveness. Ancient religious ceremonies such as the eucharist may provide this when words of assurance cannot comfort. It is also possible that restitution will be a necessary antecedent to self-acceptance. We have learned from the practice of family therapy that it is often necessary to arrange meetings between significant persons and the sufferer in order for confrontation, confession, and forgiveness to take place. It is human nature that "acts of grace" are more effective when they occur in the presence of human witnesses. Thus, we who care for sufferers are often inadvertent carriers of acceptance, grace, and forgiveness. Our faithfulness and our willingness to work with sufferers when they view themselves as unlovely, unlovable, even repulsive is often the beginning of their ability to move toward self-forgiveness and self-acceptance.

Even prayer is essentially an interpersonal activity, interpersonal not only in the sense that we speak to God, but also in that the way in which we speak to God was modeled, taught, and supported by others. Personal prayer is accompanied by memories of family or corporate prayer spoken to images of God that were shared. Thus the quality of the human support system pervades this private spiritual activity, affecting its ability to comfort the sufferer.

I close this section with a story of my Aunt Betty, who has been terminally ill during the entire time that I have been writing this book. Aunt Betty is eighty-two years old and she is slowly dying of cancer. She first became aware of the cancer when, because one hip failed to bear her weight, she fell. Upon examination, a hairline fracture in the hip was discovered. She rested, and began using a cane and walker, but the discomfort in the hip increased until it became real pain. After several examinations it was discovered that cancer had invaded the hip area. Her physicians concluded that the cancer had preceded and had been the cause of her fall. Further examination revealed that one kidney was cancerous. Treatment then included the use of radiation and "killing" the kidney by flooding it with alcohol. As the months have gone by the situation has worsened. Presently Aunt Betty weighs about ninety pounds and has a morphine pump implanted in her arm to help manage the excruciating pain. After months of terrible suffering the end is near.

But this account of the physical circumstances does not touch the real story of Aunt Betty. Aunt Betty was born in Flemish Belgium in the first decade of the twentieth century, a time when terrible poverty beset that area. In a desperate attempt to rescue his family from poverty her "Pa" came to the United States and worked for five years to save the money for his wife and five children to come to the promised land. They nearly starved until he saved the money to bring them, shaven peasants in ill-fitting garments, to Ellis Island. All they wanted was a chance to work, and work they did.

Aunt Betty grew into a woman of gracious warmth. Never having had children, she became everyone's kindly aunt. She listened well to children, slipped them occasional gifts, and always had the tea or coffee ready. She and her husband finally saved enough money to buy and successfully operate a neighborhood grocery. There her relationships expanded. She and her husband sold the business and retired to live together for eighteen years of healing closeness. What had started as a rocky marriage ended in a deep friendship.

Aunt Betty lived in the present and the future. The present was a time to be lived in warm relationship with those one loved. No day was too busy for a moment of conversation, an act of kindness, or the love of a child. She believed that the future was in God's hands. She treated her God with the same everyday consideration and friendship that she extended to all her friends. God was not simply transcendent and causal to her. It was God's business to look after her.

Less than a year after she was widowed, she discovered that she had the cancer. But this is not a sad story. Aunt Betty's years of openness and affection have left her surrounded with care. The neighbors across the street with their six children love her. Hers was their second home. Two of her nieces have provided the concern of daughters, one for her physical care and the other for her financial arrangements. In the extremes of her illness, Aunt Betty has received visitors with dignity and humor and a minimum of self-pity. Rather than wanting to get rid of her, to put her away, her extended family and friends have surrounded her with love. Despite the need for extended care, she has not spent a day outside her own home with the exception of occasional brief visits to the hospital for medical procedures.

A visit to Aunt Betty is like a reminder of how good and precious life can be. She makes one feel warm and hopeful. Soon she will be gone, but her warm memory will be treasured among her extended and adopted family for years to come. All the elements we have discussed in this chapter have been present in her life. She has had a strong sense of her own positive worth. One might say she is loaded with self-esteem. She has never overestimated or undersold her own worth. Her explanatory structure is right on the money. She has lived with a positive structure of ultimate context. Her faith in the goodness of the world and her own future has been as natural as the air she breathes. And of course, her human support structure is remarkable.

Aunt Betty has been well aware of the location and quality of professional caregivers. She has built dependable relationships with medical doctors, dentists, bankers, and spiritual advisors. She is a religious but not pietistic woman who respects her faith. She has learned that the love of God is most clearly known through caring human relationships, and she has freely given and freely received. Whether or not she is still alive when this is published will not change the meaning of this statement. She is rich in human relationships.

So this widowed and childless woman, stricken with terminal cancer, dying thousands of miles away from the place of her birth, has prepared for her death with a remarkable life. She will be missed more than mourned and will leave a heritage of inspiration for all those who have known and loved her.

Summary

I have written here of four prevenient structures that will largely determine the nature of suffering and the sufferer's response to it. The first of these, the self-esteem structure, represents the way in which we view ourselves. It includes not only those acts, images, and characteristics we see as being "me," but also the way we feel about them. Our fundamental feelings of goodness, badness, lovableness, or rejection toward ourselves are related to this structure. It is out of this structure that we predict whether other persons will love or reject us.

The second of these, the self-protective structure, represents the way in which we explain ourselves, and the nature of our existence, to ourselves and others. This structure reveals the subjective criteria for our raison d'être, the reason for our being in the world. Our goals and ambitions and the ways in which we measure our own success or failure are either implicit in, or hidden behind, this structure. The more congruent this structure is with the way we "are" and the way others see us, the better chance we will have to deal with pain, sorrow, separation, and loss in a creative and restorative manner. If our self-explanation is too defensively incongruent with reality, the crises that create suffering will come as rude surprises, and suffering will be more difficult to handle.

The broadest stage upon which we play out the drama of our lives I have called the ultimate context structure. If we live within the ultimate context of a world view that includes spiritual meaning, a sense of order and continuity, and a sense of positive direction, we are less likely to be overwhelmed by suffering.

The final structure discussed, the human support structure, is, I believe, the most self-evident.

In the next chapter we will discuss how these structures and other factors affect the emotional and perceptual foci that sufferers "choose" for their ordeals and the "nuances" of response that are chosen by different personalities; in so doing we will begin to make our focus more personal.

CHAPTER THREE

The Many Faces of Suffering

How often, oh how often,
  in the days that had gone by,
I had stood on that bridge at midnight
  And gazed on that wave and sky!

How often, oh how often,
  I had wished that the ebbing tide
Would bear me away on its bosom
  O'er the ocean wild and wide!

For my heart was hot and restless,
  And my life was full of care,
And the burden laid upon me
  Seemed greater than I could bear.

But now it has fallen from me,
  It is buried in the sea;
And only the sorrow of others
  Throws its shadow over me.

Yet whenever I cross the river
  On its bridge with wooden piers,
Like the odor of brine from the ocean
  Comes the thought of other years.

And I think how many thousands
Of care-incumbered men,
Each bearing his burden of sorrow,
Have crossed the bridge since then.

—From "The Bridge,"
HENRY WADSWORTH LONGFELLOW

The wooden piers can no longer be seen on the bridges that cross the Charles River in Boston, nor is the water brackish or tidal. A dam has been built to keep the ocean at bay. But some things have not changed. The care-laden men and women still stand and look at the reflections of their thoughts in the water. The sufferers and those who care for them still pass by.

Only a few miles from that bridge, beside a tidal cove, live two of my dearest friends. They live in their retirement home, a dream house envisioned through years of faithful service to a university in the Boston area. All the inspiration and intellectual challenge they provided for students through fruitful careers has been laid aside. Their lives have been reconfigured into a small, intense circle of love and pain. The students of pastoral care and counseling, whom they inspired, are scattered around the world doing skillful work. But my friends face the same inescapable problem each morning: how to get through another day of suffering with grace and wholeness, how not to yield to despair.

She has been comatose for almost a year now, since having surgery for a brain tumor. He manages the increasing tremors of Parkinson's disease with medication while he goes about the tender daily tasks of nursing care, cleaning, shopping, and food preparation—concrete ways of offering love to a partner who may only possibly know who he is. Loving children, with professional responsibilities, have interrupted the onward thrust of their own careers to spend great blocks of time with their parents, offering them their manual skills and emotional support. There in that "dream home," superior nursing care is being offered with tender love. It is the mother's inheritance from the many years of unself-conscious nurture, humor, and companionship she invested in her family.

This story, not as it is written but as it is lived, is poignantly bittersweet. It is indeed "the best of times and the worst of times." If the days of our own denouement were so filled with suffering, how many of us would handle it with such courage, grace, and family solidarity? Why is it that some people can bear the unbearable with dignity, strength, and courage while others surrender to despair?

What accounts for the different ways that people respond to suffering, the different "faces" they assume? Do we choose our modes of suffering or are they forced upon us by circumstances beyond our control? Can we control the directions of our thoughts, the emotional tones we assume, the styles of our response to suffering? Or is our response to suffering written into us by genetics, social conditioning, and circumstances? What are some of the variables that determine how we will respond to suffering?

Recognizing the Faces of Suffering

Suffering obtrudes itself upon us in many forms. But instead of its causing us to be more aware and sensitive, we often build a thicker defensive wall. After a while, the inchoate voice and weakened visage of suffering is so common that we hardly notice it. Suffering is a voice saying, "Do you have any spare change?" It is a figure rolled up in sheets of cardboard in a sheltered alley, a woman wrapped in layers of discarded clothing lying on the steam vents of a city street, two begrimed figures in the alley behind the brownstone where I live sharing the transitory comfort of a bottle of cheap liquor. It is a distressed mother eating tranquilizers, a harried father self-medicating with fifths of scotch, or a teenaged child contemplating suicide. These events belong to our peripheral vision. As we go about our business filled with hope and plans for the future we are almost oblivious of being surrounded by despair.

Occasionally suffering rises to the threshold of our attention. I saw a mother bedding her children down for the night on the steps of a bank building in downtown San Salvador: a family without shelter, possessions, or hope. I remember the desperate plight of a colleague who spent his

71

final years in the agony of tinnitus, unable ever to escape the intolerable ringing in his ears; and the agony of a loved one dying of cancer, almost beyond the comfort of morphine. These are some of the remembered faces of suffering. We cannot let ourselves remember all the possible visages because we cannot bear them. But, if they are so hard to remember, how can we make sense of them? I will try to raise our consciousness of such events so that we may extract some common styles of suffering from the mélange of examples we have seen.

Four Principal Styles of Suffering

Although suffering assumes many individual faces, I believe I can identify four principal styles from my experiences. In discussing these four styles, we may find the basic ingredients of many other configurations. These four styles are *suffering as apprehension, suffering as sorrow and loss, suffering as remorse and regret,* and *suffering as physical pain.* I do not conclude that these four "foci" are independent of one another, but in my work as a caregiver, I believe they are frequent modes of response.

In order to understand these manifestations of suffering, we must consider the impact of anxiety on the sufferer and the way in which it operates in the formation of symptoms of suffering. There are important psychological factors that may operate in the selection of physical symptoms. Such factors as body language, somatic compliance, hypochondriasis, and sadistic or masochistic tendencies may all influence the style of suffering "chosen" by a person—just as there may be genetic tendencies toward specific physical disorders such as allergies and asthma.

There are other factors that may enter into the question of one's "control" over the choice of symptoms of suffering. For example, what part do character traits, developed over a lifetime, play in determining one's response to suffering? What are the limits placed upon symptom choices by factors outside one's own person, such as family role models, family permission, and social acceptability? We are coming to see that certain inherited genetic and character traits seem to strap family members into modes of expression, such as panic attacks, phobias, bipolar affective illnesses, and alcoholism.

Do some ways of suffering "work" better than others as channels for the expression of pain, loneliness, and despair? In some families, being "sick" gets attention whereas being scared, anxious, or angry results in rejection. Some families seem to engender obsessional models of suffering, others more hysterical models. I remember my surprise when I was privileged to work as a psychotherapist in London for a few months. A young woman, well educated and with a responsible professional position, came to see me with a classic phobia of spiders. Although I feel sure it exists, I had never seen this phenomenon in America in persons of her sophistication. There was obviously a cultural difference in what was permissible, what would "work" as an acceptable symptom.

We may conclude that the style of suffering is determined in part by stressful precipitants (infection, accident, abuse, poverty, loss, rejection, etc.), in part by the limits and permissions of the social and cultural frames in which we live, and in part by the qualities of timing, tolerance, temperament, and character which are part of our biological inheritance.

1. Suffering as Apprehension

For many years I used an exceptionally graphic depiction of an anxiety state from Robert White's *The Abnormal Personality* while teaching a course in psychopathology.[1] The poor victim of a severe anxiety attack described his experience: A train was approaching on the other side of a small lake. As the train came through the woods the terrifying sound of it echoed through his head as if it were bearing down on him. The apprehension of this catastrophic accident was intolerable to him. He burst into tears, and began pacing back and forth and crying out loud. It was only when the train had passed safely by on the other side of the lake that he became sheepishly aware of how irrational his response had been. Irrational or not, a measurement of his autonomic nervous system would have revealed that this imagined danger resulted in a pounding heart, increased blood pressure, vascular changes, digestive inhibition, and a number of other "real" symptoms of stress.

In today's terms, apprehension is usually described as one of the symptoms of anxiety. Such terms as fear of the unknown, fear of being overwhelmed by the impulses, and fear of separation are contemporary references to states of apprehension. This group of terms, having its origin in psychoanalytic theory, has been picked up and modified by other psychodynamic theories including Object Relations theory. Although it speaks of the more emotional side of the term *anxiety*, it usually does so in a somewhat depersonalizing third-party tone. Such discussions tend to bear in mind that anxiety is basically a physiological experience.

Søren Kierkegaard used the same etymological stem, *angst*, but in a more subjective sense. He used the word to mean "apprehension" or, as it has been translated, "dread."[2] He spoke about the emotions associated with this experience in a dread-ful manner. His use of the term is closer to one's sense of being-in-the-world and is less influenced by human physiology and interpersonal relationships. It seems to me, however, that both these usages are important in understanding the role apprehension plays in suffering.

Apprehension and Anxiety

We may clear away the underbrush a bit if we briefly review the principal meanings and uses of the word *anxiety:*

1. Anxiety as a physiological problem. Eric Kandel and others have been able to trace states of anxiety to the serotonergic reactions of certain neurons. Kandel has traced differential physiological reactions for chronic and anticipatory anxiety.[3] He has suggested that the neuronal activity in anticipatory anxiety is particularly amenable to conditioning. In studies of aplysia (sea snails), actual changes in the morphology of the brain have been demonstrated as a result of conditioned anxiety.

It appears from these studies that chronic anxiety may be more physiologically based, and anticipatory anxiety a more conditioned response to the circumstances in which the organism exists. Chronic anxiety may be experienced more often as physical discomfort, and anticipatory anxiety as apprehension. Whether the stimulus for anxiety comes from within the organism, or is a result of conditioning from events outside the organism, the physical effects are clearly measurable. One interesting side note on Kandel's analysis of the literature on brain morphology and anxiety, is the possibility that, if the neurons can be changed by aversive conditioning, it is likely that they can also be changed by psychotherapy to function more positively.

2. Anxiety as a "mental" problem. Both observations in psychotherapy and research studies have demonstrated that memories and images are stored as "mediating variables" between past and present experience.[4] In human beings, stored negative images can act as triggers for anxiety at any time. The stimuli that call forth these images or memories can arise from within the person or from the environment.

Such stored "mediators" explain the manner in which responses to early traumatic experiences continue to create experiences of apprehension and physical symptoms of anxiety long years after the experiences have happened.

Many readers will remember that Freud named three principal sources of anxiety, two coming from within the person: fear of being overwhelmed by the impulses of the id, fear of punishment from the superego, and one from dangers outside the person. These he named neurotic, moral, and objective anxiety.[5] Object Relations theorists have added a fourth important precipitant of anxiety: separation. Losses, or feared losses, can generate intense separation anxiety. All of these are both biologically measurable and subjectively expressible.

What is of interest here, however, is not the sources of anxiety but the fact that apprehension can be triggered any time an unfolding situation is reminiscent of earlier discomforting events. This is particularly relevant when one is discussing suffering, since suffering can be seen as the actuation of one or another of these early fears; for example, the fear of punishment for one's "badness," the fear that life will get out of control, the fear of separation and loss, and the fear of death. One important element in affecting whether physical pain or interpersonal crises will lead to suffering is the degree to which they cause the person to re-experience such early events.

3. Anxiety as an interpersonal problem. Perhaps it is in this area that anxiety is most often experienced as apprehension. H. S. Sullivan was a key figure in helping us understand the interpersonal nature of anxiety. Jay Greenberg and Stephen Mitchell, in their book on Object Relations theory, have presented Sullivan's view as follows:

> The fly in the ointment, the hidden menace that interferes with simple living and successful integration of situations, is anxiety. The power anxiety wields over our lives, Sullivan suggests, derives from the circumstances characterizing its appearance within the infant's experience.
>
> The infant's experience of anxiety is identical to "fear." Fear is caused either by violent disturbances in perceptions (such as loud noises or cold) or by dangers posed to the existence or biological integrity of the organism (hunger or pain); anxiety, in the highly specific manner in which Sullivan uses this term, is "caught" from caretakers. He suggests that anxiety in those around the infant is picked up, even if the anxiety has nothing to do with the infant per se. The process through which anxiety is conveyed he terms "empathic linkage." . . . The anxious infant expresses his discomfort. The caretaker likewise feels tenderness and attempts to minister to the infant's needs. But with anxiety, the caretaker only makes things worse. He is the *cause* of the infant's anxiety in the first place; his attentions, although well-meaning, bring him in his anxious state closer and make the infant *more* anxious.[6]

Such a cycle of mutually anxiety-provoking relationships at a crucial age can leave the person in a bind between anxiety about loneliness and anxiety about closeness. Such a preparation for adulthood leaves the person vulnerable to both the increased need for care and the sense of being different and isolated that are so often a part of suffering.

This anxiety about closeness can especially be seen in persons with narcissistic personality problems. In the moment when they most need care and support, impending closeness creates anxiety that results in confusion and splitting. When situational or physiological crises create periods of intense suffering, such persons find that maintaining the empathic bridge is well nigh impossible. At such times, the sufferer may resort to psychosis or even suicidal gestures as a way to end the pain of despair.

4. Anxiety as a sociocultural problem. The textures of today's environments create apprehension both because they are often fraught with real danger and because they threaten the person's boundary distinctions, thus threatening the integrity of the self. Two observations are appropriate here. The first is that overcrowded environments create malaise, defeat, and despair in both persons and laboratory animals. An experiment was reported by J. B. Calhoun in which the independent variable was simply the increased numbers of rats in a cage.[7] Other variables such as the quantity of food per animal, cleanliness of cage and air, and so on were held constant. As the number of animals in the cage increased they became restive, assaultive, and withdrawn in that sequence. It has been observed that in ghetto situations human beings seem to go through similar stages in their attempts to adjust to an intolerable situation. Both loneliness and complexity create anxiety. Many urban living situations seem to contain both these problems simultaneously. It is not uncommon for persons to feel crowded but lonely, indistinguishably grouped with others but desperately alone.

If such environments are dangerous, they greatly raise the levels of apprehension in people as well. As a result, some individuals develop psychopathology while others join groups exhibiting suspicious, defensive, and hostile behaviors. Conditioned apprehension becomes a part of their lives. Such suffering often results in the use of drugs and alcohol as self-medicating attempts to alleviate personal tension.

5. Anxiety as a ontological problem. There is a more fundamental and a more universal understanding of anxiety than those discussed above. Certain forms of anxiety are indigenous to human nature. It is natural to turn to Tillich for a discussion of this "existential anxiety":

The first assertion about the nature of anxiety is this: anxiety is the state in which a being is aware of its possible nonbeing. The same statement, in shorter form, would read: anxiety is the existential awareness of nonbeing. "Existential" in this sentence means that it is . . . our own having to die that produces anxiety. Anxiety is finitude, experienced as one's own finitude. This is the natural anxiety of man as man [person as person] and in some way of all living beings.[8]

I wonder whether readers, who were not immersed in evangelical childhood religion, resonate as strongly to Tillich's words as I do. Could it be that the echoes of fundamentalist preachers, eloquently warning of the end of the world and the wrath of God to come, have served to imprint meanings that resonate to Tillich's concept of the fear of nonbeing, in my thinking? Or is it that those evangelists, who coupled the most venial sins with the possibility of eternal punishment, have simply amplified fears of nonbeing that exist in all of us by the nature of our intense early dependency and the fragility of our early efforts toward independence? It is not so much the possibility of going to hell that terrifies one, although that is bad enough, but the possibility of being cut off forever from loving support. Perhaps this is the underlying hell for all of us. Is the very development of our own selves, coupled with the diminished dependence on the godlike figures who gave us birth and sustenance, a sin of such arrogance as to threaten our very existence? Will the ultimate punishment for our narcissism, for our very success, be separation, nonbeing, and death?

This is only part of the dilemma of development. If early development has contained psychologically dangerous care-giving figures, the child may become more merger phobic than merger hungry. In support of this point, words spoken by patients echo in my ears. A lonely woman whose career was full of work and empty of persons said, "On the days when I feel good I can't let myself get close to people, because I couldn't sustain it on the days when I feel bad." A handsome young man, very ill with schizophrenia, stood with two of Albert Schweitzer's books in his hands. He said, "I'm like a glass two thirds full." And he said, "Maybe God has sent me here [to the mental hospital] to learn what it's like, so I can help other people." Each of these patients was asking in his and her own ways, "Dare I be?" "How much closeness or independence can I risk?"

An even more poignant example was shared in the dreams of a bright, sensitive male patient. This patient was a doctoral student in one of the scientific disciplines. Upon the birth of his second child, his anxiety rose so sharply that he began to decompensate. When he first came to see me, he was struggling with obsessive urges to throw himself out of an upper-story window in one of the university buildings. About one third of the way through a fairly long period of therapy, he told me of two dreams. In the first dream he saw himself as a very small child, in the home in which he lived during the first four years of his life. In the dream he was lying on a shelf near the kitchen ceiling. He fell off the shelf. "But I didn't fall all the way to the floor," he said. "It was as if I was suspended by a rope or cord and I swung back and forth between the ceiling and the floor."

"Then," he said, "I had another dream. It was as if it came through a trap door connected to the first dream." In this dream he saw women's bodies cut up and placed in a china closet in another house in which he had lived. He made me aware that it was in a rural area and that a pig may have been butchered at about the time to which the dream referred. One of the faces looked as though it might have been an aunt, his mother's sister.

So he told me the story of how he felt about his mothering. That lying on the shelf was cold and lonely, and being off the shelf did not free him but left him hanging in tangled uncertainty. The second metaphor with its mild displacement from mother to aunt, told how full of rage he was about the situation. Such thoughts, if they exist at all, must be repressed because they threaten us with nonbeing. Even the dream content must be carefully camouflaged, lest we alienate the imperfect figures on whom we must depend for our very existence. We fear nonbeing as a result of our struggles to free ourselves from dependency, and we fear that we may die if we are free. So when we view the enormous potential of our world—for relationships, power, creativity, and love—it is this very potential that may overwhelm and destroy us.

Following is Ernest Becker's clear explication of this point:

> We now know that the human animal is characterized by two great fears that other animals are protected from: the fear of life and the fear of death. In the science of man it was Otto Rank, above all, who brought these fears into prominence, based his whole system of thought on them, and showed how central they were to an understanding of man. At about the same time that Rank wrote, Heidegger brought these fears to the center of existential philosophy. He argued that the basic anxiety of man is anxiety *about* being-in-the-world, as well as anxiety *of* being-in-the-world. That is, both fear of death and fear of life, of experience and individuation.
>
> (italics mine)[9]

It is a fact of life that the moment we begin to allow ourselves to love someone, we must also begin to reckon with losing that someone. Whether it be mother, father, brother, sister, child, or lover we must bear the pain of loss more deeply if we let ourselves love. Thus even the most "normal" among us live with an undercurrent of apprehension.

Although we are aware of this fact subliminally, crises in our lives may bring it to the fore. Our own sudden illness, or that of our loved ones, instantly creates the threat of nonbeing. We may not worry about our own or our loved one's death in any clearly conscious manner, but we have a sudden sense that things can never again be what they were. Many of us have experienced that first trip to the doctor when something really different happened; a growth, sudden bleeding, loss of consciousness. When the diagnosis was given, if it was cancer, or a circulatory obstruction, or if the need for major surgery was indicated, a great dark shadow loomed across the future. It was as if a small gnawing existential cloud had suddenly darkened and increased in magnitude a hundred times.

It is just this quality, the apprehension of nonbeing, that makes suffering so horrendous. More often than not these first alarums turn out to be overamplified. Most often our physical problems, or those of our loved ones, are treatable. But apprehension has a way of making suffering seem endless. Some sufferers simply live in a continuing state of apprehension for weeks, months, or years. Medication mercifully lowers the intensity, but it may also delay or derail our efforts to solve the problem through spiritual growth and awareness. To use Tillich's phrase, "the courage to be" requires that we expand our horizons rather than shrink them; that we open up to information, rather than close our minds; that we make new relationships, rather than withdraw. It is in this sense that apprehension works against its own resolution.[10]

2. SUFFERING AS SORROW AND LOSS

The keening cry of King David when he was told of the tragic death of his son Absalom is a fitting symbol with which to open this series of considerations. As you will remember, the word of his son's death came to him as he sat at the gates to the city of Jerusalem. He was waiting to hear the results of a battle between the King's soldiers and a rebellious splinter group led by his son Absalom. The first messenger brought the good news that the attempted coup was defeated. But that left the question in David's heart unanswered. The second messenger brought the sad news that Absalom, riding a mule during the battle, had caught his head in the crotch of a tree and had died of a broken neck. The alienation between David and his son must have intensified the tragic impact of the unwelcome news. David's cry has echoed through history, "O my son Absalom, my son, my son Absalom! would God I had died for thee, O Absalom, my son, my son!" (II Sam. 18:33 KJV).

This story reminds us that suffering is inescapable for human beings. If we live long and healthy lives, dying in our sleep at the age of ninety-five, we still must face losses, losses that remind us of our own mortality, losses that cause us to lose part of ourselves. Next to dying, grieving is the hardest work in the world.

It was thirteen years ago I first learned about mortality. In that year my father and my daughter both died. The initial impact of and the continuing effect of those two deaths have been quite different. My father was a seventy-two-year-old man when he died of cancer, young for our times. But he had lived a successful and satisfying life. The nature of his illness was such that there were many visits and several significant dialogues between us over a period of more than a year. He, and we, the members of his family, had an opportunity to grieve in advance of his death, and because of the nature of his illness, to see his death as a merciful end to his suffering. There was time to speak unspoken words, and to say good-bye. Even the funeral service provided an opportunity for healing. It took place in a part of the country where a Protestant "wake" was still observed. Friends and extended family gathered around and remet one another. There was a profound sense of honoring the departed one. This was brought home to me, in a surprising way, when I saw the cars pulling off the road as the funeral cortege passed by.

The increased solidarity among members of the family has lasted to this day. I miss my father; there are things I need to say to him, questions I would like to ask. He was such a logical, competent man when it came to managing the "things" of life. Some of his tools hang in my shop, and when I am involved in some mechanical operation, I think to myself, "I guess I'll ask Dad how to do this." Of course that cannot happen, but the lessons he taught through the years have become part of me. More than money or the family name they are the real inheritance. His skills in managing employees, his orderly, systematic mind, and his unswerving determination to successfully complete tasks, are qualities, I am told, that reappear in my own life. Both the genetic inheritance and the paternal modeling are irreversible gifts. I have experienced great sadness over the loss of my father, but little suffering.

The sudden death of our thirty-one-year-old daughter was another matter. Like that of King David at the gate, our morning get-ready-for-the-day routine was interrupted by a message: an alarum. We were notified by phone that our daughter had been rushed to the hospital unconscious. She was six months pregnant and had suffered an embolism. The clot was small enough to pass through the heart muscle, but it lodged somewhere in the lungs. It was not located until an autopsy was performed. While we raced across the state by auto, every effort was being made to save her life. A team of eight medical experts worked in the intensive care unit of the hospital until it was obvious that there was no hope. She died suddenly, apparently in the best of health. Three beautiful children were left motherless—twins seven years old and a younger sister. Numbed parents and a distracted husband gathered those little children together while their father told them in unforgettably tender words that their mother was gone . . . but that we still had one another.

At first hand I watched the impact the death of their mother had on those three little girls, now young women. They had survived, but the cost has been great for them, for all of us. I found that C. M. Parkes' discovery that acute grief is experienced for about two years after bereavement was about right for both my wife and me.[11] The throbbing pain of remembrance, the initial numbness, followed by questioning, rage, and acceptance was an accurate diagram of the course of our grieving. I have written about this more analytically in another publication.[12] The most hurtful suffering has been in the lives of the three bereaved children, but that is their story to tell, not mine.

We were not prepared for the permanent hole that her death left in our lives. We were not prepared to find that thirteen years later every day has at least one silent period of loneliness. But we have learned much from this experience. We have learned that life goes on, that sorrow can be borne. We have learned that we are strong. And, a priceless insight for professional caregivers, we have learned what people mean when they talk about their own suffering.

For my own part, these experiences transformed my ability to be "with" persons who were in severe grief or life-threatening crises. I've felt much less need to "do" something for them, and much more able to be with them. I've shed such defensive caregiving protocols as introducing religious symbols or offering an assumed empathy to cover my own sense of helplessness. I am more content to wait and respond to sufferers on their own terms. They may ask for a range of responses including errands, communications to others, prayers and sacraments, listening, or help with a decision. Often they are simply grateful that I am comfortable being with them in their situations.

Losses and "Normal Abnormalcy"

Most caregivers have learned from experience that losses are among the most serious precipitants of "abnormal" states in persons. For years I heard the histories of mental hospital patients revealing one, two, or more serious losses of the important modeling or support figures from their lives. Children are particularly harmed when identity bonds are broken, when the most important figures for survival are torn out of their lives. The metaphor that I used to describe the loss of our daughter was, that a great tree was growing out of the center of my life and a bulldozer was pushing it over, tearing the tendrils, ripping the roots, destroying the work of a lifetime.[13]

At such times, all of us are normally "abnormal." We experience a defensive narrowing of perception, an assault on our own self-esteem, and feelings of guilt ("Why didn't I, I should have done," etc.). This state of mourning is routinely so severe that Freud made an effort to separate mourning and melancholia theoretically, because they looked so much alike to the observer.[14] Whether we manage such grief within normal limits and recover within a "normal" period of time, or become emotionally ill, depends on some of the factors that were discussed in the last chapter. It is certainly true that the loss of loved ones is a major precipitant for unusual behavior in "normal" persons and that it can trigger serious emotional illness in persons whose emotional health is shaky to begin with. "Normal" people can become withdrawn and socially myopic. They can respond with anger when friends try to reinvolve them in life. They may become anhedonic (pleasureless), or sexually promiscuous in an effort to hang on to life. They may not wish to see any of the persons who were part of their lives with the deceased, and they may exhibit many other "normally bizarre" behaviors.

Some sufferers simply cannot recover from such losses without professional help. It is relatively common to see some forms of affective illness triggered by the loss of important loved ones. I have seen both major depressions and manic episodes occur after the loss of a husband, wife, or mother. In other persons, "neurotic" problems are triggered. Phobias, anxiety states, or conversion symptoms are not uncommon. If such cases are treated with a combination of medication and psychotherapy the recovery can result in the resolution of problems that have needed attention for years. We will discuss caregiving for persons suffering from losses in chapter 5.

When Dreams Die

There are losses, other than the death of loved ones, that can trigger severe stress. The effects of separation and divorce can be very severe. Separation often means loss of support, relationship, and physical closeness. A divorce often results in prolonged loneliness and problems with finances and child-care. It may also be seen as the final rejection, delivering a terrific blow to the person's self-esteem. At such times the person may feel lonely, needy, enraged, and undesirable all at once. A divorce is the death of a dream, a dream in which partners have invested years of their lives and much of their money and energy. Sometimes partners, who have long since exhausted their ability to relate to each other, who may even hate each other, cling to their marriages because they cannot bear to give up the dream. It is common to see separation and divorce trigger clinical depressions. At best there is bound to be sadness, anger, loneliness, and a long period of recovery from this "normal" grief.

The loss of meaningful employment is another principal source of stress. Vocational dreams often die slowly, causing severe problems in adjustment. There is great human tragedy around plant closings, leveraged buy-outs, and extensive administrative shake-ups. It is particularly difficult to be unemployed while others prosper. Lowered self-esteem, loneliness, and feelings of failure are common. If unemployment continues, suffering and despair are almost inevitable. Sleeplessness and other anxiety symptoms are normal results of prolonged unemployment. Clinical depression and thoughts of suicide can easily occur in cases where support systems and ego integration are fragile to begin with.

Physical Illness and Loss

A severe sense of loss takes place when one's body is altered by accident, surgery, or disease. We have spent a lifetime building a familiar concept of our physical selves, our "body images." Our sense of well-being is so geared to the image of a functional organism that most of us feel a bit depressed or angry if we are impeded by influenza, the common cold, or a sprained ankle. It isn't just our bodies that feel miserable, it is our whole attitude toward ourselves. This becomes more profound if the changes in our bodies are life-threatening or severely image-altering. Here too a dream is lost. The dreams of youth, vigor, self-sufficiency, love, and success may all be under attack. The problem becomes still more profound if the nature of one's illness interrupts support relationships, leaving one to live and die away from those one loves. Sadly, the AIDS epidemic has made such tragedies commonplace.

Losses, whether of loved ones, of dependable and useful physical functions, of lifelong images of our own bodies, or of dreams of good marriages, loving children, and accomplished goals, are the stuff of which sorrow and suffering are made. Later we consider ways in which such losses can be, at least partially, overcome.

3. SUFFERING AS REMORSE AND REGRET

One of the most dramatic stories recounted in the Bible (John 8:3-11) was that of Jesus confronting the crowd gathered around the woman caught in adultery. One pictures this scene as a model of self-righteous chauvinistic projection. The self-appointed judges and executioners, about to stone the life out of the adulterous woman, were mostly males. There is no mention of the man who might have been sexually involved with the woman; she stood alone as the object of the moral rage of the mob.

A similar scene was depicted in the movie *Zorba the Greek*. The widow, who had held herself away from the sexual advances of the men of the town, was stoned to death on the church steps when it was discovered that she had spent the night with Zorba's friend and employer, the Englishman. The lust of these men, many of whom were married, was transformed into self-righteous, maniacal rage. It was as if their troublesome inner impulses were projected onto the widow, in an illusion that they could be smashed to death along with their object.

In the biblical story, Jesus rescued the woman from her accusers, forgave her sins, and rebuked the members of the mob for their hypocrisy. As the woman teetered on the edge of death the tether on the mob's fury began to weaken when Jesus penetrated the dramatic moment with one terse statement, "Let him that is without sin cast the first stone."

According to the story they "began with the eldest to go away." One wonders if they were recounting the litany of their sins as they turned away. If so it may have been an illustrious list. Although the dramatic focus of the story is on the widow's plight and her rescue by Jesus, it is the relationship between guilt and rage that is of interest here. Turned outward the guilt became rage, destructive enough to take a human life. When Jesus redirected the guilt inward, it turned to shame, and the fury of the mob fragmented into individual self-loathing. This fits the time-honored psychoanalytic view of depression as rage-guilt turned inward. Hagop Akiskal and William McKinney have reviewed major theories of depression and summarize:

For those in the psychoanalytic tradition, depression represents the introjection of hostility resulting from the loss of an ambivalently loved object.

87

The Abraham-Freud model views depression as the inward turning of the aggressive instinct that, for some reason, is not directed at the appropriate object. The retroflexion of hostility is triggered by the loss of an ambivalently loved object. . . . This model is phrased in metapsychological terms and does not lend itself easily to empirical verification.[15]

While they go on to review more modern theories of depression involving object loss, cognitive structures, and neurochemical functions of the brain, this theory seems to fit both the story recounted above and the experiences of many sufferers.

It makes assumptions about lost innocence, and its relationship to aging, that may apply to all of us. It seems to assume that sins, and their memories, accumulate as one grows older. If this is true it could be concluded that the older one becomes, the deeper the residue of accrued remorse and regrets. The words *remorse* and *regret,* translated into theological terms, can mean sorrow for sins against others and against ourselves. Remorse is the sorrow we feel for having hurt others. It may be the result of unknown unselfishness, social insensitivities, socially approved competitiveness, of our own hostility. Most of us accumulate a list of omissions and aggressions a tender conscience will ultimately review.

We also accumulate a list of regrets. These are the memories of all the things we meant to do—the places we meant to go, the things we meant to see, the kindnesses we meant to offer. This "I never sang for my father" syndrome haunts many persons to their graves. Lost opportunity, lost potential, and undeveloped friendships are part of the underdeveloped self that shadows our existences. This too may have been masked by the vital lie of our lives with its pattern of achievements and material possessions. But the heart knows whether we have been true to our best selves. It is when illness or aging interferes with one's ability to compensate, when hope for redressing one's moral balance sheet is interrupted, that one becomes preoccupied with one's failures or sins.

Pushkin's poem "Remembrance" makes this very point:

THE MANY FACES OF SUFFERING

When the loud day for men who sow and reap
  Grows still, and on the silence of the town
The unsubstantial veils of night and sleep,
  The need of the day's labor, settle down,
Then for me in the stillness of the night
  The wasting, watchful hours drag on their course,
And in the idle darkness comes the bite
  Of all the burning serpents of remorse;

Dreams seethe; and fretful infelicities
  Are swarming in my overburdened soul,
And Memory before my wakeful eyes
  with noiseless hand unwinds her lengthy scroll,

Then, as with loathing I peruse the years,
  I tremble, and I curse my natal day,
Wail bitterly, and bitterly shed tears,
  But cannot wash the woeful script away.

—ALEKSANDER SERGHEIEVICH PUSHKIN

Captured in Pushkin's poetry are experiences familiar to many sufferers. When the diversions of the day are past and the busy cacophony silences itself, and while others sleep, there are many who lie awake recounting their sins, faults, and errors. Some of them recite a well-worn, often recalled, litany. It is as if a button in the brain had been punched, bringing forth a pretaped record of past mistakes. Others re-create painful scenes replete with emotionally loaded imagery, reliving, as they remember, the painful, pleasurable, loving, sorrowful, guilty, or regretful feelings that remain part of those memories. Both the intensity and repetitiveness of such memories are profoundly affected by one's level of self-acceptance. When we feel generally good about ourselves we can balance memories of past failures by focusing on present successes. If we feel good about ourselves we can remember our faux pas with humor and grace. But if we are suffering from illness, handicapping conditions, or the limitations of aging, these memories may become tragic rather than humorous.

These nocturnal maneuvers are easiest to understand when they are part of grief or depression. Grief states are often accompanied by obsessional repetitions: having failed the loved one, having been slighted or abandoned by the loved one, having been let down by the caregivers who let the loved one die. Thus rage and guilt become commingled in these distressing thought patterns. Though painful, in normal grief they are temporary.

States of depression are also often accompanied by obsessions. As Marie Kovacs and Aaron Beck have pointed out, these repetitions often consist of "the negative cognitive triad," that is, negative thoughts about the self, the world, and the future.[16] These repetitive thoughts both help and hinder. To feel that finally one's basic inferiority has been uncovered, that finally one is being punished for one's secret sins, or that finally one's basically negative view of the world is being proved true, is to have, at least, some explanation for what is happening. Such thoughts are attempts to retain structures in one's life, to keep even more frightening ideas and feelings from breaking through one's defenses.

But these maneuvers limit emotional growth and problem solving, making it almost impossible to get insight into one's situation. They work against positive change. Any intervention that breaks the cycle and broadens the view can be helpful. If the support of family and friends is not enough, appropriate medication, psychotherapy, and, in extreme cases, electroconvulsive therapy may be used to interrupt obsessional thoughts, thus allowing healing to begin.

In discussing remorse and regret we encounter a theological question. That question, framed by Karl Menninger, is: "Whatever became of sin?"[17] It is easy to deal with "depressogenic thoughts" by making psychological or structural analyses of their nature in the mode of the cognitive therapists.[18] Psychoanalytic theory has become such a *lingua franca* that an understanding of repeated negative thoughts resulting from a rigid punitive superego is within the grasp of most lay persons. Most modern therapists attempt to alleviate the effects of such negative thoughts by helping the patient connect them to relative social values. The support given by the therapist, along with the broadened view of social mores, tend to diminish the self-punishing thoughts. In addition, the patient is helped to uncover experiences that may lie at the core of "neurotic" problems, so that the experiences may be treated in a less frightened and more rational manner. Punishment, loss of control, and other feared results do not occur as the material is uncovered. Thus, the patient learns to live more comfortably with the uncomfortable material, having "relativized" it by confessing to the therapist, and to his or her self, and receiving the absolution of continued acceptance.

Both Karl Menninger and Hobart Mowrer disagree with this scenario.[19] They believe that confession is being made to the wrong person. Running contrary to "scientific" opinion, they suggest that really hurtful actions lie repressed at the core of our neuroses, the alleviation of which requires confession, and perhaps restitution, to the persons wronged. Within a theological framework, there are at least three injured parties when we sin: God, those whom we have sinned again, and ourselves, whom we have hurt most of all. In a theological sense, we have damaged our relationship with God, injured others, and disappointed ourselves. The theological cure for this state of affairs is expounded in Judaic and Christian theology and in the theories and practices of many other religions. Confession, restitution, and divine forgiveness lie at the core of most of these methods for restoring persons to a state of "grace."

These "theological" methods for being forgiven have found their way into modern therapeutic practice in several ways. Family therapists have learned that extended family conferences, often intergenerational in composition, enable confession and forgiveness to take place. This opens communication and restores trust so healing can take place.

Alcoholics Anonymous has long used a simple theological formula in its successful practice: recognition of one's sinful state, appeal to a "higher power," confession of one's sins, and membership in a faith community.

The self-alienation that occurs when we fail to live up to the calling of our better selves ("ego ideals") is recognized by the humanistic psychologists. Their use of the principle of self-actualization to explain the movement of human beings toward a more complete explication of their own natures is, for me, a thinly masked and poorly stated principle of teleology. Within theological understandings, the self-actualizing instinct of human beings is simply an echo to the call of God's Spirit to higher levels of being and relationship. This seems to me to have been developed much more explicitly, and scientifically, in the writings of Teilhard de Chardin.[20]

This longing for fullness and for completion survives to the end of life, even when the sufferings of age and illness have diminished one's power. Even death can be embraced as a friend ushering one into a final stage of growth. As Imara has written,

We abhor and reject the moment when we will confront the nearness of our death. But the dying stage of our life can be experienced as the most profound growth event of our total life's experience. The shock, the pain and the anxiety are great, but if we are fortunate enough to have time to live and experience our own process, our arrival at a plateau of creative acceptance will be worth it.[21]

Even with greatly diminished powers and damaged intellectual facilities, our longing for confession, forgiveness, and unity with God seems to exist. Many times, religious rituals such as prayer, the Eucharist, or the Seder are redemptive metaphors that still exist within the ultimate context of the sufferer. These symbols may hold when illness has affected judgment and rationality. It is a good thing for all of us that our salvation does not depend on our ability to "figure things out." In this regard, one of the last conversations I ever had with my father remains deeply etched in my memory.

My father, European immigrant that he was, came from the "spare the rod and spoil the child" school. Since I was the eldest child, having come at a time when he was least experienced as a parent, punishment was often generously corporal. During the last stages of my father's terminal illness with cancer, the children and grandchildren gathered from across the United States to meet, eat together, and say good-bye. As I was about to leave the gathering, I knelt beside the end of the sofa where my father was seated. In the course of saying good-bye, the subject of those childhood whippings came up in the following manner.

"We're going to leave now Dad. I just wanted to tell you that we love you."

"Even if I knocked you around?"

"Dad, I forgave you for that long ago."

"I didn't know much about raising kids; I thought you had to knock them around."

Thus did my father, after years of quiet remorse, emerge from behind the well-respected facade of dignified strength, to take care of a small but important piece of spiritual business. He didn't need to be told that I loved him, or to have our basically good relationship reaffirmed, but he needed to confess his "sin" and be forgiven. I suspect that he had long since discussed this matter with his God.

This dialogue does not take away the memories of a child, overwhelmed by power and pain, wondering what he could have done to deserve such severe punishment. But it does leave one with a mellow sense of acceptance and equality. Somehow it helps one to feel that in the long turnings of the world there are moments of grace and justice. It is a reminder of how often we who care for sufferers are conveyors of acceptance, grace, and forgiveness. Often we are stand-ins for deceased, unresponsive, or overly terrifying figures who cannot be approached by those who suffer. Our faithful willingness to work with sufferers when they feel unlovely, even repulsive, may be the beginning of a spiritual healing that includes forgiveness, acceptance, and heightened self-esteem.

4. Suffering as Physical Pain

One of the great secrets in our culture is the nature of physical pain. It is inexpressible when we are caught in its grip, and unrememberable when we are not. It defies empathy, because the moment we begin to express it, we create defensive responses in those who listen. Even we ourselves find it hard to remember the experience of pain between its episodes. Therefore we are apt to remain amateurs in the understanding of pain. I feel that this is true of myself. I know something about the physiology of pain receptors, the neural conductors of pain messages, and I have observed the wonders of modern pain medication, but my own experience with physical pain is limited. Although there have been several broken bones, a few episodes of gouty arthritis, and a few pulled muscles, most of my experience is limited to a period in my late adolescence when, as a student in a religious boarding school, far from home, I was taken by three plagues.

The first of these was a plague of adolescent sexual urges, which turned out to be indigenous to my time of life, problematical in terms of morality and action, but nonfatal and temporary. The second was a plague of carbuncles on the back of my neck. These uncomfortable menaces, likely caused by too many carbohydrates and obstructed hair follicles, yielded to growing maturity and departed permanently.

The most serious plague was an attack of dental decay. Having been away from home-cooking and dental surveillance for about three years, I was attacked by cavities. The dentistry of that day was rudimentary by modern standards. No root canals were attempted; several jaw teeth were peremptorily pulled with "groanings which cannot be uttered." But the real sources of pain were the "jumping toothaches" that throbbed in the night and the antique drills that were used to effect repairs on the sources of pain. I can still feel those drills vibrating against the bony structures of my head when I think of them. The sound was all-encompassing. It closed me into a private world of intolerable apprehension. The occasional searing pains that occurred when the drill reached nerves that had not been anesthetized left me with trauma regarding dental care for most of my natural life. Even in such serious matters there is redemption. I have since become acquainted with the miracles of self-cooling high-speed drills, dentists educated in T.L.C., and the wonders of modern anesthetizing drugs; it's a whole new ballgame. Yet those pains and terrors approached despair and created a fair amount of empathy for pain sufferers.

But these experiences are trivial when compared with the pain of arthritis sufferers who experience years of recurrent aching in their joints. I have visited persons whose gout was so painful that the bed sheet could not be tolerated against a swollen toe, and persons hospitalized with dermatitis whose whole bodies were covered with a swollen, suppurating rash. The pain of burn victims is legendary. When the skin, the largest of bodily organs, is extensively involved, the pain seems unbearable. Many caregivers have seen the ravages of cancer, heard the moans of pain, and seen the terror in the eyes of the sufferers.

Pain Is Hard to Communicate

Our relationship with pain is mostly inferred, rather than experienced, and even the pain we have experienced ourselves tends to be either inexpressible or forgotten. In her recent book, Elaine Scarry captured this idea:

Whatever pain achieves, it achieves in part through its unsharability, and it ensures this unsharability through its resistance to language. "English," writes Virginia Woolf, "which can express the thoughts of Hamlet and the tragedy of Lear has no words for the shiver or the headache. . . . The merest schoolgirl when she falls in love has Shakespeare or Keats to speak her mind for her, but let a sufferer try to describe a pain in his head to a doctor and language at once runs dry." True of the headache, Woolf's account is of course more radically true of the severe and prolonged pain that may accompany cancer, or burns, or phantom limb or stroke, as well as of the severe and prolonged pain that may occur unaccompanied by any nameable disease. Physical pain does not simply resist language but actively destroys it, bringing about an immediate reversion to a state anterior to language, to the sounds and cries a human being makes before language is learned.[22]

Upon reading this, one is immediately struck by the loneliness of pain, because one's suffering is unique to oneself and because there is no language with which to share it.

The Earliest Expressions of Pain

It is in the relationship with the earliest of objects that pain is first experienced and expressed in prelingual form.

During this primitive stage, the infant seems to alternate between being painfully overwhelmed with discomfort and blissfully satisfied with comfort. The beginnings of any sense of object-beyond-oneself have to do with the first great caregiver, the mothering one. The first object relationship was so bonded and unitary on the one hand and unexplicated on the other that Heinz Kohut has coined the word *selfobject* to indicate its psychological interpenetration.[23] It is in this merged preverbal stage that we first learn to experience and report on pain. These first communications are mostly physical: oral but not verbal. They consist of vigorous crying accompanied by wriggling, twisting, and throwing one's hands and feet about. To the observer, they seem to be a combination of physical discomfort and emotional terror.

Since they are so totally involving, I have called these responses "organismic." They are ante-nuanced in nature. If the reason for the discomfort is not soon ministered to, the child moves into what appears to be a panic reaction, turning red all over while weeping and threshing about. In this sequence, there seems to be both a conditioned terror response to pain and a tendency to canalize responses to pain at a preverbal level.

It is easy to see why a language of pain is so limited. Pain first occurs when object identity is incomplete; the child is in a preverbal state, and the mothering one may be as apt to respond empathically to the infant's discomfort with touches, murmurs, and neologistic utterances as with words. When we consider the fact that "pain" can as easily be "psychological" as "physical" the identification and communication of pain become even more complicated.

The old "mind-body" convention is not very helpful in understanding these relationships. When it comes to human beings, everything is potentially "mental," and mental is inseparable from the activities of the brain. Modern research has increased the ability of physicians to alter mental states by using medication that changes the action of neurotransmitters within the brain.[24] Anxiety states, mania, depression, and psychotic states have all responded to such medications. But these medications also tend to muffle rather than explicate pain.

We have all observed that behavior becomes more regressive when one is ill. Ranging all the way from busy executives to neglected elderly parents, illness provides an excuse for regression. It provides one of the few social permissions to be weak and helpless. It allows us to be unashamed while others take care of us. This is often accompanied by a sloughing off of the hard won accoutrements of independence, competitive success, and consensual modes of communication. Language and habits change, words become simpler, the tone of voice changes, and one is permitted to *be dependent.* Under such circumstances it is not easy to get the sufferer to tell what is wrong.

Pain Is Culturally and Familially Specific

The very permission to have pain varies greatly from family to family, and from culture to culture. In *The Challenge of Pain,* R. Melzack and P. Wall have commented on this problem:

A vast amount of study has been devoted to the perception of pain, especially in the last decade, and from it is emerging a concept of pain that is quite different from the older views on the subject. The evidence shows that pain is much more variable and modifiable than many people have believed in the past. Pain differs from person to person, culture to culture. Stimuli that produce intolerable pain in one person may be tolerated without a whimper by another. In some cultures, moreover, initiation rites and other rituals involve procedures that we associate with pain, yet observers report that these people appear to feel little or no pain. Pain perception . . . is a highly personal experience, depending on cultural learning, the meaning of the situation, and other factors that are unique to each individual.[25]

The authors then describe the hook-hanging ritual, practiced in parts of India, where the celebrant goes about suspended by metal hooks pushed under the skin of his back while he blesses the children and crops of certain villages. Other practices, such as lying on nails or walking on hot coals, appear to depend on the participants' attitude toward pain to avoid damaging physical consequences. The opposite of this is to see persons tearfully reporting excruciating pain that baffles medical detection.

The Measurement of Pain

Despite all these complications, considerable progress is being made in developing instruments to locate and measure pain. Melzack and Wall, after examining all the major research on pain, decided that any effective theory of pain must account for the following:

1. The high degree of physiological specialization of receptor-fibre units and of pathways in the central nervous system.
2. The role of temporal and spatial patterning in the transmission of information in the nervous system.
3. The influence of psychological processes on pain perception and response.
4. The clinical phenomena of spatial and temporal summation, spread of pain, and persistence of pain after healing.[26]

In 1965 Melzack and Wall proposed a new theory called the "gate-control" theory of pain. Following is their brief description of this theory:

The dorsal horns of the spinal cord act like a gate which can increase or decrease the flow of nerve impulses from peripheral fibres to the central nervous system. . . . When the amount of information that passes through the gate exceeds a critical level, it activates the neural areas responsible for pain experience and response.[27]

Using this theory, Torgerson and Melzack devised the "McGill Pain Questionnaire." In doing so, Melzack recognized that conventional medical usage of such terms as "moderate pain" and "severe pain" related to just one dimension of pain: intensity. It was obvious upon listening carefully to sufferers that there were other dimensions. Scarry described how Melzack approached this problem:

When heard in isolation, any one adjective such as "throbbing pain" or "burning pain" may appear to convey very little precise information beyond the general fact that the speaker is in distress. But when "throbbing" is placed in the company of certain other commonly occurring words ("flickering," "quivering," "pulsing," "throbbing" and "beating"), it is clear that all five of them express with varying degrees of intensity, a rhythmic on-off sensation, and thus it is also clear that one coherent dimension of the felt-experience of pain is this "temporal dimension."[28]

They were able to arrive at a "thermal" dimension and a dimension called "constrictive pressure." From these, they were able to develop more overarching categories such as the "sensory," "affective," and "cognitive" content of pain, thus providing a theory that would organize oral comments about experiences of pain into types. This instrument has assisted patients in expressing the nature of their pain more accurately, and has assisted physicians in locating the physical sources of pain. Using the words "searing," "pulsing," and "shooting" tells the physician that the patient is referring to thermal, temporal, and spatial dimensions of pain.[29]

The Thresholds of Pain

From the theory, it is clear that "pain" messages must reach a certain cumulative level, a "total pain threshold," before the "neural areas" in the dorsal horns of the spinal cord "activate" to pass the message along to the brain. These messages may arise from physical trauma resulting in pain (such as injuries, accidents, inflammations, etc.), or they may arise from emotional stress created by events outside the body. How does the brain sort these out after they pass the "threshold"? A few comments from Nancy Andreason's book *The Broken Brain* may help clarify this point:

When we are confronted by a major stress, which may be psychological (as when a loved one dies) or physical (as when we are in an automobile accident), this information is perceived and felt by our brains. Recognizing that we will need extra resources of energy and alertness to cope with the stress, the brain sends a message to the hypothalamus telling it to stimulate the pituitary to release more cortisol. . . . The adrenals then pour out cortisol, and information about the amount of cortisol in the bloodstream is sent back to the hypothalamus, which is sensitive to plasma cortisol levels. . . . Thus the whole system is regulated by a set of feedback loops.[30]

The important point to be made here is that messages other than those indicating physical pain can alert the same system to danger. Perceived danger, such as that which plagued poor Tom in chapter 1, can have the same effect. The fear that one may be condemned to eternal punishment can have the same effect. The fear of the loss of support by important human beings in one's world can also trigger the system. Thus, experiences of pain, while all are mediated by the brain, may arise from spiritual and interpersonal as well as physical sources.

In determining what is painful to the person, all these sources of suffering must be considered. Does pain signal intolerable physical suffering, separation from important support figures, loss of self-esteem, altered body images? Does pain indicate the loss of spiritual meaning? It seems clear that pain usually receives additional loadings from one or more of these sources, and these either amplify or mitigate its effects. It is also clear that the treatment of physical causes of pain is not, in itself, sufficient.

One observes, in caring for persons suffering from physical pain, that their tolerance thresholds vary greatly from one time to another. From the physical point of view, pain often seems to worsen in the evening. Some combination of fatigue, imminent aloneness, and letting down defenses seems to contribute to this phenomenon. We seem better able to handle pain when we are more rested, have time to plan for it, are surrounded by support, have appropriate distractions, or feel better about ourselves. Physical pain is also less tolerable during longer periods of stress, loneliness, or financial emergency.

In concluding this examination of suffering as pain, it is important to remember that the causal loop works in the reverse direction as well. Nonphysiological stress can cause physical pain. We often use the peptic ulcer as an example of this. Although more recent medical understandings of stomach ulcer emphasize physiological and genetic causes, it is clear that ulcers are greatly exacerbated by emotional states. But whatever the causes, the physical results are real. Most physical illnesses are affected by the emotional states of the sufferers.

Why Sufferers Sometimes Choose Pain

For both admirable and "neurotic" reasons, persons sometimes choose to be in pain. The last days of Sigmund Freud were an example of the former. Having finally obtained permission from the Nazi government to leave Vienna, where he had been a captive in his apartment, Freud moved to London. But within a year he had a recurrence of the cancer that had seemed to be in remission in Vienna. Faced with increasing pain and an ugly cancerous ulceration of the cheek and the base of the orbit (the eye socket), he refused any medication except occasional aspirin. Biographer Ernest Jones has described the situation:

Freud, like all good doctors, was averse to taking drugs. As he put it once to Stefan Zweig, "I prefer to think in torment than not to be able to think clearly." Now, however, he consented to take an occasional dose of aspirin, the only drug he accepted before the very end. And he managed somehow to continue with his analytic work until the end of July.[31]

Freud, so affected by cancer that the odor from his ulcer drove his beloved dog, a chow, into the corner of the room, chose to continue his labors in intense pain rather than lose the mental clarity that would allow him to work by sedating it away. At great cost to himself, Freud chose to feel fully human as long as possible. His courage in the face of death has gained him considerable respect, even among his detractors.

At the other extreme are persons who need to be ill, who welcome pain for pathological reasons. Listed in the well-used *DSM III* is an illness called Munchausen syndrome, described as follows:

The person's entire life may consist of either trying to get admitted to or staying in hospitals. Common clinical pictures include severe right quadrant pain associated with nausea and vomiting, dizziness and blacking out, massive hemoptysis, generalized rashes and abscesses, fevers of undetermined origin, bleeding secondary to ingestion of anticoagulants, and "lupuslike" syndromes. All organ systems are potential targets, and the symptoms presented are limited only by the person's medical knowledge, sophistication, and imagination.[32]

It is clear that such patients needed and "used" illness for their own psychological reasons.

Perhaps a more common phenomenon occurs among patients experiencing decompensation during the onset of mental illness. I can remember patients, ridden with anxiety, who were engaged in a desperate search for a physical illness. They would sometimes run through a series of symptoms in an attempt to discover what was "wrong" with them. The relief on their faces was palpable when they believed they had discovered the real physical cause of their strange and frightening feelings. It was obviously less frightening for them to be "ill" than to be "crazy."

As it turned out, there was indeed something wrong physically. Researchers have discovered that neurotransmitters in the brain can malfunction and that medication can correct this. I was still working in the hospitals when the first widely used neuroleptic drugs, reserpine and chlorpromazine, were introduced. These drugs, since replaced by more refined medications with fewer side effects, produced some of the most dramatic positive changes in human behavior that I have ever seen.

But Munchausen syndrome and the desperate search for physical illness among those experiencing emotional or "mental" breakdowns are not the only examples of the desire for pain. Examples of masochism as part of sexual practice are as old as literature. Several theorists have explained the conjoining of sexual and hostile aims (sadism) and sexual and self-punitive aims (masochism) as means to sexual gratification. Both psychoanalytic and Object Relations theorists offer convincing explanations of how such "distortions of aim" become established in the development of some human beings. For many persons, pain, within bearable limits, is pleasurable.

But examples of the painful pleasure of being hurt exist outside the sado-masochistic paradigm. Self-punishment seems to serve two purposes. The first and most obvious, is to act toward oneself as an external superego. If we can punish ourselves in the place of the feared authority figures whose images we have internalized, we may be able to accept and love ourselves. Freud's description of the unbalanced way in which the conscience is formed remains classic to this day. He described the superego as the "legatee of parental authority," which has "taken over the power, the aims, and even the methods of the parental function." About that he wrote:

The super-ego seems to have made a one-sided selection, and to have chosen only the harshness and severity of the parents, their preventive and punitive functions, while their loving care is not taken up and continued by it. If the parents have really ruled with a rod of iron, we can easily understand the child developing a severe super-ego, but, contrary to our expectations, experience shows that the super-ego may reflect the same relentless harshness even when the up-bringing has been gentle and kind, and avoided threats and punishments as far as possible.[33]

Unfortunately, this tendency to shape the images of authority figures as punitive and demanding extends to internalized images of God as well. Some religious systems lend themselves to this distortion of the nature of God. The sense of God as providing a teleological pull toward more completeness, toward higher levels of development, is completely missing from some religious systems, while beliefs in inherent evil support punitive self-images. This is a developmental tragedy, because visions of oneself as "good" and lovable are important to healthy development and are undercut by such points of view.

Self-punishing behaviors have appeared as aspects of penitential practice in religious sects from time to time. These pain-inflicting measures in the forms of whipping, stretching on the rack, lying on beds of nails, and so forth, have been used for both sadistic and masochistic applications. In the light of today's theology, and in the light of what we are learning about the positive developmental results of good Object Relations, it is hard to reconcile any conception of God with such primitive behaviors. It seems that anyone's God would be more interested in the formation of positive ego-ideals, coupled with the support and acceptance needed to reinforce behaviors leading to success and self-esteem.

In primitive personalities, such self-punitive behaviors as beating one's head against the wall or superficial slashing appear to be efforts to administer punishments that will make one acceptable to poorly internalized authority figures. Both hysterical characters and borderline characters seem to be given to such behaviors. Such behaviors often occur as "transference" reactions in the course of therapy with patients with these diagnoses.

I believe there is a second reason for the self-inflicted pain often seen in primitive personalities. When mentally retarded persons were still kept in huge hospitals, I observed what seemed to be repetitive self-punitive behavior by some of the patients, including hair pulling and deep scratching. It is possible that such acts were done to get attention or to express rage. It seemed to me, however, that they were simply ways of reifying existence. In situations where object relationships had no chance for richer development, this primitive, uncognitive relationship patients had with themselves and in which they were narcissistic objects, at least proved they were alive.

Children during the first year of life may be seen pulling their hair or chewing on their feet as a normal way to establish boundaries between "me" and "not me." The reference points for such children were not solely narcissistic since many environmental objects such as balls, bottles, blankets, feces, and more were tested by biting, chewing, and banging to establish their "me," "not me" categories. But in testing out the limits of our beings there is a sense in which even pain makes us know that we are real.

Embracing and Using Pain

Not long ago a friend and her husband visited his mother, who had recently suffered a stroke. Upon arriving at the facility where the patient was being cared for, they made several observations:

1. The physical recovery from the stroke had progressed surprisingly well. Although speech was somewhat slowed and flat there was no evidence of aphasia, apraxia, any serious problems in the cognitive process, or any seriously impaired mobility.

2. Emotions were more labile than usual, with easily triggered weeping.

3. There was an imperious dependency on caregivers. This extended to the point where the patient would not use her good hand to pick up the water glass, but called a caregiver to hold the glass while she drank.

4. All efforts to walk independently had been abandoned. Some use of a walker was made in the immediate living quarters, but any movement outside this limited space was done in a wheelchair.

5. The physician in charge of the patient assured the family that the patient's mind appeared to be functioning well for her age and that there was no reason she could not resume mobility.

There appear to have been two principal motives causing the patient to decide to be an "ill" person. The first was the normal fear of further accident or damage. The second seems to have been a more powerful reason and was what the psychoanalytic literature calls "secondary gains." A lonely woman with a lifelong narcissistic need to be special, and a basically imperious personality, fell into a set of circumstances that allowed all those dynamics to be expressed. She was suddenly the center of attention, with "servants" at her command. In one fell swoop she found herself surrounded by persons important to her and with renewed power over their lives. She was in no hurry to get well.

The reader will not be surprised to learn that she made wonderful progress during the protracted visit of her family members. They poured out love and support, using both

105

affection and logic to get her moving again. Having demonstrated the seriousness of her plight during the first few meetings, she was willing to exchange illness for love, and slowly regain her independence.

"Illness" and the Identified Patient

A young woman in a rural area lived with her loving, controlling family, and this family had very conservative principles. When she became sexually mature she developed a paralysis and spent several years in bed as an "invalid." Finally a professional caregiver who recognized the symptoms of hysterical paralysis came into contact with the family. This happened when the young woman suffered a physical problem that required medical attention. An intervention was made that separated the young woman from the family, moved her to a hospital, and initiated psychotherapy. After a number of supposedly caring intrusions by her family, the young woman aborted therapy, returned to the family home, and resumed being an invalid.

Needless to say, there was nothing physically wrong with her. The whole family had colluded around this patient, accepting her willingness to sacrifice her autonomy, freedom, and growth rather than deal with the feelings that might have been unearthed during her recovery. Despite the fact that there is often a terrible price for everyone in the family to pay, individuals, even families, will choose to be ill. In such cases it is clear that the treatment of psychological and spiritual illnesses is the first step to wholeness. It is also clear that individual sufferers often cannot get well, if the system surrounding them is unhealthy.

If sufferers who have chosen to be ill are to relinquish their symptoms, the trade-off must be worthwhile. Illness can be exchanged for support, relationship, love, or opportunity. It will not be exchanged for loneliness and despair.

Summary

In this chapter we have discussed the universal nature of suffering. We have recognized that the conditions which cause suffering may spring from pain in one's body, from memories and images stored in one's brain, from stresses in one's relationships, and from losses. We have tried to deepen the reader's insights into suffering by presenting four principal descriptive categories: suffering as apprehension, suffering as sorrow and loss, suffering as remorse and regret, and suffering as physical pain. These categories were enlivened by the stories of real human beings. They were selected to heighten our understandings of the sufferer's experience, using theory and "scientific" evidence to highlight experience, rather than to prove our case.

The informed reader will have recognized that there are "diagnostic" categories running close to the labels we have used. Such terms as *depression, guilt,* and *anxiety* are close relatives of *sorrow, remorse,* and *apprehension.* I have intentionally avoided diagnostic categories since they imply psychopathology. I believe that many healthy persons experience the types of suffering I have described, and I believe that all these descriptions can be recognized by the reader as patterns in the tapestry of his or her own life. I have given attention to what might be happening in the sufferer's relationship with himself or herself, his or her family, and with his or her conception of God.

We have explored the developmental history, psychodynamics, relationships, and images of the sufferer, and we have tried to experience with the reader what the texture of suffering is like. It is my hope that we have experienced not only the tragedy, but also the richness of suffering. My purpose here was to share a sense of hope, respect for those who care for sufferers, and belief in growth in the midst of adversity and pain.

CHAPTER FOUR

Overcoming Despair

This chapter will introduce the stories of Sinclair, Ted, and Sarina, three memorable players on the stage of life, in whose dramas I played a small part. These three teetered on the brink of despair and came back. I shall write of the two men first and then of Sarina, whose story has a different backdrop, different causes and results, and sings with its own poetry.

As I think of the two men, educated members of upper middleclass families, both with good manners, community respect, and better than average financial resources, I am reminded of Edwin A. Robinson's familiar poem "Richard Cory."[1] Written during the years of the Great Depression, it paints the picture of a man who masks his silent despair, his inner torture, behind an attractive social facade. A man who is the model of success to the laboring people of the Depression era, even while he lives in his own cavern of secret pain:

> Whenever Richard Cory went down town,
> We people on the pavement looked at him:
> He was a gentleman from sole to crown,
> Clean favored, and imperially slim.
>
> And he was always quietly arrayed,
> And he was always human when he talked;
> But still he fluttered pulses when he said,
> "Good-morning," and he glittered when he walked.

And he was rich—yes, richer than a king—
And admirably schooled in every grace:
In fine, we thought that he was everything
To make us wish that we were in his place.

So on we worked, and waited for the light,
And went without the meat, and cursed the bread;
And Richard Cory, one calm summer night,
Went home and put a bullet through his head.

Sinclair

When I first saw Sinclair he wore a yachting cap and drove around town in a used Bentley. There was a quality of decadent elegance about him. He was like a tuxedo with a slightly raveled sleeve, a cravat slightly worn at the knot. His manners, always proper, had a quality of reserve that made one feel a bit looked down upon. Quite intentionally, I believe, this rakish facade masked the warmth, intensity, humor, and occasional rage that lay beyond his surface presentation of himself. His intelligent face had a slight distortion as if Bell's palsy were tugging at the corner of his mouth. It was much later I learned this was a memento from a youthful attack of polio. All in all, Sinclair seemed like an intriguing, mysterious, solitary, and distant figure to me.

It was after he contracted Guillain-Barré syndrome that I really got to know him. Then I discovered a person of unexpected depth, sensitivity, integrity, and courage. But let's let Sinclair tell his own story:

I was in my forty-first year when the neurological disorder known as Guillain-Barré syndrome struck me. The year was 1977. I had recently begun work as an administrator and teacher at the local high school. By Thanksgiving, I was exhausted and run down by my new job. My resistance was low and my anxiety level, which had always been a problem, was high. I came down with bronchial pneumonia right after Thanksgiving and was admitted to the local hospital. While in the hospital, I began to develop the unusual symptoms of numbness and lack of feeling in my hands and feet. Also, my balance was becoming unsteady when I tried to walk. I lost control over my bladder function in that I could not urinate and had to be catheterized. My physician correctly diagnosed my strange symptoms as Guillain-Barré syndrome, a virus which attacks the sheath around the nerves and destroys many nervous system functions.

... by Christmas my condition had deteriorated to the point where I was hooked up to the life support systems in the intensive care unit at University Hospital. My impressions and memories of those weeks in the intensive care unit ... was of being in a sort of dream-like state of semi-awareness. Yet, if it is not a contradiction, I was totally aware because impressions of that time remain very vivid in my mind and will always remain an important component of my psyche as long as I live. I think I was aware that I could die, but I do not feel that I was particularly afraid of this. I almost feel as if I might have been unconsciously preparing for this to happen.

Despite this seeming tranquility of mind, I was physically and emotionally suffering and in a state of trauma; that I know. I was physically helpless and totally dependent on others for all my needs. Perhaps this was the most emotionally painful and frustrating part of the early experience—this feeling of helplessness and a concomitant feeling of hopelessness which grew stronger as time progressed. Anger grew into rage as the weeks progressed and as I was actually improving very slowly. The "why me?" question was further compounded in my case since I had gone through an equally serious illness, Polio, some thirty years before—and now here it was, happening all over again.

The rage was great enough so that I did not yet find much time for depression although I am sure that I was very depressed as well as being angry. There were some fleeting thoughts of "Just let me die"—a passive suicide urge, although I do not feel that the urge ever became active in terms of making an attempt on my life. It was more a feeling of "F—— this life and f—— mankind—I want no more part of it." In retrospect, it seems somewhat strange to me that I was most serene in my outlook when I was most seriously ill in intensive care and then became more angry, frustrated, and enraged as I slowly began to improve. It was almost as if I had been cheated of death and had to start dealing with a painful recovery and its consequences.

This story arouses a response in me, as I record it, that is almost painfully empathic. It is as if Sinclair is presenting a prototype of what I understand suffering to be. The understanding of suffering with which I concluded chapter 1 was written long before I received Sinclair's self-descriptive letter. Yet there is a strange congruence between his account of his suffering and the definition of suffering in chapter 1:

Suffering is a nearly unbearable state of human existence arising from stress or tension in any part of the human interactive system—physical, psychological, interpersonal, or social and spiritual. It is more related to the duration than to the intensity of emotional or physical pain. As stress continues over time it may cause confusion, loss of self-esteem, a sense of meaninglessness, and finally despair. The person involved may lose faith in himself or herself, God, the future, and positive human values. Deep cynicism, emotional withdrawal, or even suicide may result from the sufferer's attempt to escape from hopelessness.[2]

The principal elements of suffering seem to be present in Sinclair's description of his experience: damaged self-esteem, diminished hope, a sense of potentially endless duration, intense loneliness, profound loss of meaning, and mounting despair. During the "intensive care" portion of his illness, he seems to have been able to use a combination of dissociation and dependency to buffer himself from the enormity of his situation. The terrifying alternatives—dying or living to be less than his full self—were distanced through hope for recovery and the safety of being cared for. He literally gave himself over into the care of others, thus pushing the enormity of the life-versus-death dilemma into the shadows. In many ways it would have been easier to die without having to face that decision.

But then he discovered that he was not going to die from the disease after all, but must reassume responsibility for his life. If he was to live he must fight back. It was at this point, with both energy and physical equipment limited by the ravages of the disease, that he began to feel hopeless and enraged. Life seemed both burdensome and meaningless as he was forced to assess the residual damage from his illness. Listen to his account of this period of his recovery:

By February of 1978, I was strong enough to be transferred from University Hospital to Regional Rehabilitation Hospital where I would spend the next five months, until June, recovering, recuperating and being "rehabilitated" through physical and occupational therapy. . . . I still could do very little for myself. I could not sit up for more than ten minutes without exhaustion, nor could I feed myself, nor go to the bathroom independently. . . .

One of the most painful and unpleasant parts of my existence in 1978 was having to be catheterized, and then learning how to catheterize myself. Since the fine motor control in my hands and fingers was poor—and it is still so today so that I type most everything rather than write—it was very painful and tedious to do the catheterizing two or three times a day. It also obviously restricted my going too far away from my equipment . . . I was either in the hospital or house-bound. . . . My bladder function did return on its own with little or no warning. I was at my father's house in Sarasota, Florida on my first major venture out of my house. This was my last major recovery of a lost function as I have never recovered my balance.

It was after Sinclair's return to his "home" that my deeper relationship with him began. Actually he did not return to his own house since it was not yet equipped for a person with a handicapping condition. Instead, he was able to rent a very attractive and comfortable house equipped with ramps, railings, special bathroom equipment, and the like. I had had several caregiving roles in the neighboring communities, having been pastor of a church, academic dean of a college, and a human relations consultant to industry. At the time I received Sinclair's call asking me if I could visit him, the major focus of my work was a private practice in psychotherapy. When I knocked he called out for me to enter the house. I found him in a pleasant bed-sitting room area toward the rear of the house. As he reintroduced himself and began talking about his situation he was pleasantly polite, but his voice quavered and his hands shook.

I soon began to see how frightened he still was. He was frightened by two awful possibilities: that he would not recover further and that he would survive within a limited and useless existence. After giving me a "bare bones" history of his illness, he told me how depressed he had been feeling, revealing that this included some disturbing dreams and fantasies of suicide. After an appropriate period of sizing up the situation, and each other, we decided to work together, thus beginning a professional relationship that lasted about three years. My training as a clergyperson made it easy for me to make "house calls," and I continued to see him in his home on a weekly basis until we terminated therapy.

During the period of our work together, Sinclair had regular visits from a physical therapist and received a great deal of help from social services in general. In the early months I would support him in his discouraging efforts to use the parallel bars, fix a cup of tea, or pour a glass of water as adjuncts to our therapy sessions. I soon discovered that the afferent nerves to his lower limbs were seriously impaired. Although his sensorium in this area was pretty good, he simply did not have expressive muscle control and has never since regained it.

Our work together unfolded naturally; there was a period of relationship building, his present dilemma was empathically accepted, and the "life story" was told. This story included his birth into an affluent family, which lived in the "old money" area of an Eastern city. The story of his immediate family included affluence, social position, and tragedy. Perhaps it can be summarized by saying that his mother took her own life, his brother had been diagnosed as having a thought disorder, and his father was a financially reliable, distantly caring figure. Sinclair had the advantages of a fine private-school education and the disadvantage of always having been alone, even in the midst of his family.

It seemed to me that he felt he was haunted by ghosts of the past. He was concerned about a dark side in himself, sometimes ruminating about the possibility of chronic depression and eventual suicide. But he was blessed with a wonderful sense of humor, often using dark humor as he looked ruefully at himself and his situation. When I first met him, Sinclair gave an accurate picture of his emotional range in describing his five months in the Regional Rehabilitation Hospital:

There was an extremely mixed bag of emotions with which I had to deal during this time running the gamut from despair, hopelessness, cynicism, pessimism, depression, anger, rage to short interruptions of encouragement, humor, joy, hope and laughter. I think that my sense of humor helped me to keep a realistic perspective on things and certainly helped me to keep my sanity.

For me those "short interruptions of encouragement, humor, joy, hope and laughter" were evidences of ego strength upon which the future might be built. I worried, along with Sinclair, about how much of his physical functioning and therefore his life could be recovered. But I soon came to know him as a bright, determined man who, with help, was willing to face the worst of his situation. We did uncovering work as needed but focused mostly on ego supportive therapy. We focused on repairing his damaged self-esteem, not with platitudes of encouragement, but by reflecting demonstrable progress in his relationship building and recovery of physical competence.

We rejoiced together when he had his first nocturnal emission since his illness signaling to him that his sexual functions had returned. We faced the fear of learning to drive again. It took months before he was willing to have a car equipped so that it could be driven without foot pedals. The first few trips out with the driving instructor were terrifying for Sinclair. He quit for a while, worked it out in therapy, and went back to the lessons. When he regained the skill and courage to venture forth into the world in his new car, I felt that he had become reengaged with life.

He began to understand that as long as his mind worked well and as long as he could receive and communicate information, he had a vocational future. Sinclair may never know how much I admired his courage when he pointed that adapted automobile toward the nearest graduate school and earned a second master's degree in counseling. Over time there was a gradual emotional shift with more frequent periods of sunshine and a generally more positive attitude. The therapeutic method included much listening and acceptance, some hands-on help, some uncovering and insight, and a good deal of discussion of practical ways to manage life. Sinclair arranged to have ramps, easy access doors, and a swimming pool built in his own house so that he could enjoy the only vigorous exercise his muscles could manage. He was then truly able to go home again.

Sinclair has no glowing inspirational story to tell. His courageous recovery and his vital reengagement with life are sermons that glow without words. Although in some ways he remains skeptical and disenchanted, his current thoughts are filled with wisdom, hope, and better insights:

I feel that I have become more patient and tolerant in many ways and understanding of other people's suffering and their vulnerability. But, I have also become less patient and tolerant and more outspoken of those I perceive as fools for one reason or another. My impatience here borders on contempt. An example of this might be any religious zealot or fundamentalist. I do not suffer fools lightly—or, those I perceive as fools.

I think that this was always latent in my family and my upbringing, having come from an upper-class, white, traditional, genteel, Gentile, WASP, East Coast Establishment, preppie, Ivy League, Anglophile family. Disgusting isn't it. I was brought up with an unspoken but understood perception of the world as belonging to my class and people and that one must be polite and understanding, and *try dahling* to understand and humor the unfortunate masses surrounding one. Noblesse Oblige. This attitude is an insidious, insufferable, intolerance which I luckily have fairly well shed, although not completely. The irony is that my family is just as screwed up, if not more so, than many of the "great unwashed." The privileged position has led to some nobility, but also much tragedy. . . . I see no grand scheme of things as far as mankind is concerned. If there is a scheme, it is in the cosmos and is not to be comprehended. Man is insignificant and somewhat ridiculous in his pretensions and religions—"a poor player who struts and frets his hour . . . ." The human condition is both comic and tragic, but not so important as we would be made to believe. I favor the comic side with the fool as protagonist, and it is an acute sense of this human comedy which has endowed me with a sense of humor and a fairly sharp wit. This philosophical and intellectual view has been my saving, amazing grace which most likely has helped me to continue to live, and to fight recurrent bouts of depression.

. . . the feelings expressed above have been . . . covered over by an "optimistic" or "cheerful" persona and world view. The illness helped me to shed this mask and to express a healthy skepticism concerning myself and man's world in general. This feels more natural and honest to me. . . . Although I obviously wish that this catastrophic illness had never happened to me, it has helped me to shed some false and foolish facades.

I still find life to be interesting, and seem to keep busy and not be bored. . . . I have no trouble relating to people of all kinds, and seem to have always had the knack of liking and being liked by others.

115

Despair is always on the horizon. I do not rule it out, but for now I seem to have adapted to my condition and to have weathered the storm as best I can. However, we are all fragile and potentially vulnerable so I rule out nothing in the future.

So we take our leave of Sinclair, his honest words echoing in our minds. I find myself incredibly touched by his willingness to share his pain, disillusionments, and partial triumphs with me, and because of his trust in me, with you. This act of trust rises above his residual cynicism, above his hurtful family history. It seems to me that he offers to share his life with us in the hope that it may reduce our suffering, so that we too may survive the worst of times.

Sinclair ended his story by writing, "There is no grand scheme. One can only live day to day until one passes to the infinite."

I experienced Sinclair as a compassionate man. Hidden behind his cynical facade was gentleness and concern that outweighed his angry narcissism. In the process of our work together, I was aware that he cared about life, believed in the possibility of growth and healing, and was willing to trust our relationship. Although he is careful to limit his affirmations of the goodness of life, lest he tempt the gods, he does allow the possibility in his writings that the scheme may be grander than we know. When he suggests that he will live a day at a time and then pass into the "infinite," there is a feeling that he may secretly mean "The Infinite." It is as if he plays out his life against an Ultimate Context he does not publicly claim or pretend to understand.

I wonder if Sinclair ever knew what a "fool" his therapist was. I foolishly believed that his healing was the work of God and that "healers" are "instruments of God's peace" as Francis of Assisi suggested. Further, I believed that both the resilient nature of human physiology and the skills of the psychotherapist were part of a "grand scheme" (to use Sinclair's words).

It may be that I believed for both of us. I certainly had a sense that Sinclair was a valuable person who had the potential for important contributions to the ultimate humanness of us all and that whether we succeeded or failed, he was well worth the effort. I felt, as I often do, that we were working within the realm of Ultimate Being and that we were being called, together, to greater wholeness. Sinclair's recovery supports my belief that the greatest growth occurs in the environment of caring relationships. I confess to an experience of awe that I always feel in the face of great courage. There is something beyond the causal expectations, beyond the actuarial data in Sinclair's recovery. There were emotional and spiritual qualities in Sinclair himself, toughened by a life of disappointment, that helped him survive circumstances that could easily have destroyed him. It is these qualities that one calls upon and reflects back to the patient in the midst of his or her despair. And it is from such persons as Sinclair that we therapists derive the strength, the "faith," to begin the journey with other sufferers.

A POSTSCRIPT TO SINCLAIR'S STORY

Having written the words above, I visited Sinclair, personally, to give him the opportunity to critique what I had said about him. Our correspondence had been through the mail and by phone; thus, I had not seen him personally for about five years. I was pleased when he expressed appreciation for the accuracy of my presentation of his situation, requesting that I not change a word. During our brief and pleasant visit, two events occurred that made things I had written about him seem almost "spooky."

When I arrived at his comfortable mountain view home, we exchanged warm greetings and I left the manuscript for him to read, promising to return in about an hour. Having completed a few small errands, I returned and we settled down to talk. He said, "I want to play something for you!" Whereupon he wheeled his chair over to his stereo system and punched a button. The room was flooded with Simon and Garfunkel's rendition of "Richard Cory," one of the songs from the album *Sounds of Silence*. Sinclair told me that "Richard Cory" was one of his favorite poems, and that he

117

had used Simon and Garfunkel's record to interest his high school students in the poem when he was still teaching. He said that the poem was an almost perfect metaphor for the way he had felt about himself.

After we finished discussing the manuscript, he shared some of his current activities with me. Among the community involvements that he had accepted were research and writing for a local publication, service on local committees and boards, and some "getting out the vote" political activities. He then showed me a program he had prepared for his funeral service, if and when it should be needed. It was composed of beautiful classical music and readings. It included specific prohibitions against christological language with a request that God be addressed as "the Great Spirit" or "the Infinite." Finally, he picked up a book from beside his chair and told me that he had been reading daily from the writings of Francis of Assisi. I thought he might already be transforming the "infinite" into "The Infinite."

As I drove back toward the city I felt a sense of comfort about Sinclair. Not only did he seem gentler, warmer, more self-accepting, and more involved in life around him, but also he had made progress in defining the Ultimate Context for his life and preparing with reasonable comfort for his own death. This preparation of his funeral service had none of the qualities of a death wish about it. He appeared rather as one who was planning to "wrap the drapery of his couch about him and lie down to pleasant dreams."[3]

The Story of Ted

Ted has asked me to write his story for him. He has always hated paper work and deadlines. In fact, the story emerged as we ate breakfast together in an inn overlooking a waterfall. I had told him during an earlier telephone conversation that I would like to use his story as part of a book. To provide an appropriate context, and to reassure him of the professional and ethical integrity of my intentions, I brought a couple of completed chapters with me. He glanced at them casually,

118

put them down, looked me directly in the eyes, and said, "I trust you." So, you will see Ted through my eyes, presented as I think he would see himself.

Ted was the eldest of three sons born to educated, upper middle-class parents. He spent his childhood living at private boys' schools where his father was a respected teacher. The manners and social structure of the private school, with its sense of privileged propriety, Bass shoes, and corduroy suits, were second nature to him. To complete the picture, he was a devout Episcopalian, whose belief in God and attendance at Sunday worship were more than *pro forma*.

In the summary of his recovery from Guillain-Barré syndrome, Sinclair wrote: "I tell people, somewhat tongue-in-cheek, that I am still a WASP-AE, but that the initials have changed from Anglo-Episcopalian to Agnostio-Existentialist."

Such is not the case for Ted. He is the kind of person upon which the best of the Establishment is built: mannerly, courteous, involved in his community, true to his beliefs, and faithful to his God. Add to that a quality of compulsivity, which keeps him striving no matter how joyless the task, and a quality of passive aggression that keeps him outwardly civil no matter what the inward distress or rage, and you have the phenotype of Ted. These qualities were thoroughly established early in Ted's life. He was three years old when his next younger brother, Sammy, was born. According to Ted, his mother's remark at that time was, "I don't need another child; I have a perfect child in Ted." When I first met him these qualities were still in place, but with serious cracks showing in the facade. Upon closer contact, he turned out to be both a more interesting and a much more distressed person than he first appeared to be.

This apparently "ideal" family was haunted by tragedy. Sammy, who seemed to his older brother to be Mr. Everything, who was socially and vocationally successful with an attractive wife and young daughter, died suddenly and tragically. After a period of shock and grief for the whole family, Ted, acting in what appeared to be a heroic manner, married his brother's wife and assumed the care of his young niece. Thus he became even more deeply embroiled in an intensely oedipal family structure. Soon thereafter twin girls were born to this union.

His youngest brother, Roger, whom Ted called the "brightest of us all," became the family rebel. He acted out against his family and the Establishment in predictable, self-destructive ways for a number of years. To quote Ted, Roger was "thrown out" of the private boys' school, where his father taught, in the middle of his senior year. He finished the year in a public high school and went into the Army. He was then "thrown out" of the Army. Having had a lifelong struggle with his sexual identity, he came out of the closet after leaving the Army, announcing that he was gay. He worked for a while at a fairly menial task in a public service agency to get his bearings, and then decided to finish an undergraduate degree so that he could study for the ministry. After final examinations were over one semester, he and some female students decided to drive to the ocean, which lay two hours away, to watch the sunrise. Roger, who was driving, fell asleep at the wheel and was killed.

When his father called Ted to inform him of Roger's death, a forbidden thought flashed through Ted's mind, "Now it's all mine!" And indeed it was; the family inheritance, his brother's wife and daughter, and all the complex aspirations and distortions of the family descended upon him.

His marriage, bound for catastrophe, reached its destined crisis within a few years. In Ted's words, "She made my life miserable in many ways for years."

His sister-in-law, now wife, needed more intensity, presence, and confrontation in marriage than Ted could tolerate. As she intensified her need for contact, becoming more demanding, he became more passively resistant. Finally, his rage, and the need to defend himself from intensity, took the form of sexual impotence. On his wife's part, there were episodes of sexual acting out and one wrist-slashing incident. These were stormy antecedents to the final crisis.

In desperation Ted left home, the couple formally separated, and divorce proceedings began. As the time approached for the decree to be final, in which he had agreed to forfeit custody of the children, he felt more and more depressed and agitated. In his own words, "I couldn't stand losing the children, I was afraid the kids would be destroyed by the divorce."

About a month before the date of the final divorce proceedings, a genuine melodrama occurred. On a day when his wife and daughters were out of town, Ted mowed the lawn at the home the family had shared together, then returned to his bachelor quarters where he "drank wine by the tumbler full." At eight o'clock in the evening, he returned to the family home and as a dramatic final gesture he played *Cavaleria Rusticana* over and over again. He then wrote three letters of farewell—one to his parents, one to a close friend, and one to his children. Then, according to Ted's account, he took "about fifty" tranquilizers. He then went out to the barn in his drunken, narcotized state, and attempted to hang himself. Apparently the barn was used for overflow sleeping accommodations because in the midst of all this "somehow the mattress caught fire." The neighbors in the village saw the smoke and called the fire department. They found Ted with the rope around his neck slowly sinking under the waves of alcohol and medication.

He was rushed to the hospital and placed under careful medical surveillance overnight. When it became obvious that he would survive, he was transferred to the psychiatric unit of University Hospital where he spent a month. There he refused tranquilizers when they were prescribed for him, and while he wanted to be dead, he "had no more thoughts of killing myself." After release from the hospital, he had follow-up sessions with two different psychiatrists and a few months later sought me out for more extended therapy.

The question lingers about whether Ted was intent on killing himself, or whether he simply let a dramatic cry for help get out of hand. The answer is now irrelevant, but the margin between life and death was paper thin. A few more pills, a longer delay in getting to the hospital, an accident with the rope and this story would not have been written.

When I first saw him, Ted presented himself in a polite,

tight, affectless style. He told his story in a flat, obsessional manner leaving little opportunity for his own feelings or for the therapist's response. Beneath his courteous demeanor there was a mass of heavily controlled rage. As is often true of human beings, Ted presented a complex "layered" personality. His lifelong training as a "good boy" was like a nylon fabric that held his personality together. He was socially appropriate, faithful to commitments, active in his college alumni association, and faithful to the Episcopal church. He was always attentive to his mother, before and after his father's death. But below that "good boy" surface was a defensively vigilant, intelligent, calculating, and witty persona. His humor, often on the dark side, was an outlet for acidic references to persons he did not like, and for caricaturizations of negative qualities in persons he did like. In looking deeper, there was a well of rage, seething at the betrayals he had experienced and, even deeper, wounded sorrow that he simply could not touch.

His natural politeness, along with his therapist's compassion and acceptance, made it possible for us to be together week after week. His compulsive personality style guaranteed his presence at the therapy sessions, and I, as his therapist, was ready to participate in the struggle with him, no matter how dysphoric the mood or repetitive the content.

The transformation of Ted was incremental; there were no great leaps. Slowly, trust was established and pain emerged, slowly wounds were healed, slowly new relationships were made, and slowly his personality became more spontaneous and effective. Such a relationship teaches anew what caregivers must remember, that is, that patient listening and acceptance, the ability simply to "be with" the sufferer, lies at the core of the helping relationship. In Ted's case there was a frame of family and religious values within which this growth could occur. Although there were many "neurotic" qualities in the family history, many hypocrisies and disappointments, the family itself was consistent and predictable, providing a "steady," albeit painful framework for understanding Ted's life.

This entire structure was under stress when I first met him.

Although he had attended church faithfully throughout his life because he "always wanted to be there," he had given up church attendance because he was "blaming God for the divorce." He was immobilized by love-hate ambivalence toward all the important figures in his life. As therapy progressed and the wounds slowly healed, he forgave his ex-wife for uncovering his inadequacy, he forgave his mother for controlling him, his brothers for dying, his father for not having been stronger, God for letting him down when he most needed help, and finally and most improbably, himself for having been such a failure in his own eyes.

Today, Ted smiles more often. He looks forward annually to the visits of his young adult daughters, generously providing assistance with their travel and education. He lives in a graceful home, an authentic example of the architecture of its genre. He has been remarried for several years and has made a positive vocational change. He is active in the affairs of his community, his college alumni association, and his church. As he said in our conversation by the waterfall, "Being a Christian means, partially, corporate worship." In these and other ways he belongs to persons and structures that he loves. All of this, it seems to me, is a marvelous alternative to suicide.

Only he knows how often the ghosts of the past intrude into this scene. Only he knows whether those bleak landscapes of despair still flash before his inner eye. But as I met him and shared an almost sacramental breakfast with him, gently recapturing his story, I was flooded with gratitude for the goodness of life that gives so many of us a chance to live again, more fully.

Sarina's Story

I will begin Sarina's story in the middle, and in her own words. She wrote them under the heading "Description of Despair."

I literally felt my situation was without hope; I felt surrounded by total darkness; there was no light at the end of the tunnel. Basically,

123

I could see no reason to go on living. I wanted to withdraw from people. Physically I was extremely slowed down.

One day in this condition I saw my doctor, agreed to let him call the mental health unit of my local hospital and say I was coming in. I didn't. Instead I bought a nylon rope and drove to a wooded area in Vermont; made a noose, hung it in a tree that I could get up into. I put my head in the noose and stood there thinking, I have no idea how long. In that place I found a reason to live: my two children and the fine small town we lived in. I left the noose hanging there and called a friend who came and met me. I stayed all night at his home and the next morning he and his wife took me to the hospital.

What is it that leads a gifted, educated person, deeply committed to good manners and Christian principles, to such an ultimate moment of decision about living or dying? How does a person with such obvious merit, from a good family, with a mother, sibling, and children who love her, arrive at such a terminally desperate moment? As I came to know Sarina better, it seemed to me that many of the causes were situational and social rather than developmental and familial. Granted, there were elements of depression in her biopsychological nature; and some of her self-critical perfectionism may have been modeled and conditioned in her family environment. But social stereotypes about women, chauvinistic religious structures, and the pressures of organized religion toward narrow, stereotyped avenues for sexual expression played a central role in the depressive illness that almost cost Sarina her life. As you will see from her story, Sarina's greatest problem was being a woman; a woman with an other than socially "normative" sexual identity, living in a chauvinistic culture. I have asked Sarina to speak herself. Since the material she wrote for this book is in outline form it will be necessary to fill out the text at times, but wherever quotations occur it is her story in her own words. The brackets are mine:

Crisis creating events. (I don't know how far back to start). A dear friend a year ahead of me at a women's college taught me love-making (she hasn't wanted to see me in recent years; does she feel guilty?) My first physical excitement with a man was on shipboard going to Europe the summer after I graduated from college (no intercourse).

In seminary [actually a graduate department of religion] I allowed myself to be used by a classmate for masturbating him. He had quite a reputation with the women for offering us rides home and stopping on the way.

I met a man a class behind me in seminary who was "on the rebound" from an engagement broken by his fiancée. (This is no fun remembering.) My [younger] sister was engaged to be married in the springtime. Robert [the man on the rebound] wanted to marry, I think, because he believed churches wanted a minister who was married, and I felt some pressure to get married because my younger sister was (terrible reasons for doing it!). So we became engaged in my senior year. As I was writing engagement announcements, I got a letter from the chairperson of the Religion department at my college asking me whether I would be interested in teaching there after I graduated. . . . I now often wonder what my life would have been like if I had accepted that offer.

So, Sarina's marriage, a marriage of convenience to fulfill social expectations, began. The reasons for such marriages are complex and overdetermined, yet they often beckon as antidotes for loneliness and as symbols of normalcy. In the long run the decision is simple; such marriages seem better than the alternatives. Writer Maya Angelou, who understood such things, spoke of such a marriage in a scene between herself and her mother.

"Do you love him? I admit I'd find that hard to believe. But then I know love goes where it's sent. . . . Do you love him? Answer me."

I didn't answer.

"Then tell me why. Just why are you going to marry him?"

I knew Vivian Baxter appreciated honesty above all other virtues. I told her, "Because he asked me, Mother."

She looked at me until her eyes softened and her lips relaxed. She nodded, "All right. All right."[4]

Sarina's first sexual experience with her husband occurred on the wedding night. For the first six years of the marriage, she was "reasonably happy." She finally got pregnant after trying for three years. She writes:

I seemed to feel that I had to have a baby to prove to others and myself that I was capable of doing so. I had bad nausea for four months; our first daughter was born.

During my second pregnancy, Robert began to develop a romantic involvement with a woman in the church where he was minister of Christian Education. It was kept very quiet. I played the "understanding" wife for a long time. Our second child was born.

I confided in a woman from the church who was older than me. She was married, and I initiated a romantic relationship with her. One of the biggest crises was the day she told me that I had taught her to be a Lesbian. I went home and cried the rest of the day. Robert wanted to know what was wrong. I thought about whether or not to tell him for several hours, and then did.

We went to different counselors. I may have gone first . . . to a Presbyterian minister [pastoral counselor] in a neighboring town. My main memory of him is that he always managed to place himself so that I couldn't shake his hand on entering or leaving! He had training in counseling, but seemed very uncomfortable.

Robert went to a psychiatrist. He became very depressed. His doctor told him he was angry. One night I felt he [was trying] to rape me; I became assertive and resisted. Another night we were in bed and I told him (again) that I wanted to teach. He said he didn't want me to. I said why not? He said because I'd do a better job than he did (as a minister). I said who would know? He said he would. He got out of bed and went downstairs. Then I heard the car start and realized the garage door hadn't gone up. I ran downstairs and found the door to the garage locked; so I got an umbrella and broke the garage window and then called the police.

In a few weeks or months a man from the congregation went to the senior minister and told him that Robert had made advances to his wife . . . this was a different woman from the one Robert was already involved with. That was it; he lost his job and we moved. He promised not to see the first woman any more. Eight months later I found out he did, asked him to move out, and we separated. The children and I moved to New England. Two years later we got a divorce.

Sarina was hired as a teacher in a reputable private high school. She moved to a charming New England town and established residence for herself and her children. During this transition she kept touch with her family of origin (her mother and sister), who were supportive of her. But she was faced with a new and lonely environment, new financial and house-care responsibilities, and the management and care of her two children. Her story in her own words continues:

I did fine for the first several years in my new location and new job. Rather suddenly then, I felt a strong need come on me for a close relationship with an older woman, and at the same time realized that I needed some counseling. I went to a friend, a widow, who was very warm and helped me find a counselor, a man, another minister in a city about an hour away. I saw him at least once a week for several years. He saw my bisexuality or Lesbianism as a sickness and tried to change my attitude about it.

During all this I leaned heavily on my new friend [the widow]. I told her about my strong feelings for her. She always listened and was very accepting of me, but always said a firm no to any physical-sexual relationship with me.

I became very depressed. I remember dreaming that I was a sheep and the fence around the pasture was closing in on me. To me that [dream] represented my doctor's trying to change my very nature. I started trying to figure out how to commit suicide. I told him that I was thinking of hanging myself. He smiled and said something like, "That wouldn't work unless the knot was on the left side of your neck." I told him I was thinking of driving into the rock walls along the interstate highway. He said something like, "That probably wouldn't kill you; it would just ruin your car."

Then I noticed that there were places along the Interstate, before it crossed a bridge over another road, where one could drive off into the median strip to the left of the bridge and the car would fall down onto the lower road. I told him I was going to do that. He seemed to take me seriously for the first time. I believe he called the highway department because *later* fences were put up in those places to stop cars from doing just that.

It was soon after the discussions with her therapist above that Sarina bought the nylon rope and stood in the crotch of the tree deciding whether to jump off and hang herself. She looks back on the brief hospitalization that followed as having been very helpful to her. She was placed on antidepressant medication, which helped to stabilize her. When she finally returned to her therapist, the relationship was no longer viable.

From her own story above, it appears that Sarina was enraged and disappointed both because of her therapist's cavalier responses to her suicide threats and because of his conventional views of sexuality, which appear to have made empathy difficult, if not impossible. She began looking "extensively" for a new therapist, preferring a woman. And she found one, a good one, according to her account. The woman was a psychiatrist whom we shall call Dr. Cioffi. Here is Sarina's account of this relationship:

I felt good about the work I was doing with her. But six months after I began working with her, she told me she was going to be moving to California in several months! She also said she would not have taken me on as a patient if she had known at the time she was going to move. I was saddened by this as I felt what I will call an unbiased acceptance by her. Perhaps I felt this because her attitude seemed in contrast to that of the two pastoral counselors who, though they tried to be impartial, seemed to reject either me or my sexual orientation.

It was at this point that Sarina entered my life. She impressed me as being intelligent and truthful, but chronically anxious, depressed, and suspicious of relationships. There was a sense of primitive animal survival about her. She had been deeply hurt and disillusioned and was carrying a load of unresolved rage toward her ex-husband as well as resentment about the dependent needs of her children. She was markedly lacking in joy, spontaneity, and positive expectations. She had no love life and was literally dying for intimacy. The blunting effects of continuing medication were also obvious. No doubt the medicine had been a best alternative and had served a useful purpose, but it was fast becoming a crutch. Over the few years before I began working with her, she had had three therapists, a brief hospitalization, and had been on medication for more than a year.

We established a clear structure for the relationship and engaged in ego-supportive therapy with incursions into developmental, family, and marital history as these became appropriate. It was obvious that the "self" needed corrective regrowth within the framework of a trustworthy and empathic relationship. There were two aspects of her life that especially needed to be respected. She was a person of thoughtful religious and human values who should not be insulted by cliched or superficial responses to her search for personal meaning. She was also engaged in a great struggle between the orthodox religious and family values that had helped hold her life together and the dawning discovery that at her deepest level of identity she was a lesbian. Simply stated, she was struggling to discover whether she and her God could respect and accept a self that was put off by sexual intimacy with men but longed to be united with women.

As is always the case, the human beings in her life including her family, clergypersons, and academic colleagues were the un-selfconscious mediators of God's acceptance and ultimately of her own acceptance of herself. There still remained, despite her disillusionment and anger, a strong base of religious faith and a great wish to be useful in the Ultimate Context within which she framed her life.

Sarina made remarkable progress in therapy. She was soon off medication, and at the end of our two years of working together she was markedly more positive in her attitude toward herself and her life. Her rage had abated and she was able both to be less dependent in her relationships and to be more assertive, no longer functioning on the margin of her emotional capability and ego strength. She had sought out a woman's support group and had begun to make new and positive relationships with women. At that point we terminated therapy with a couple of sessions scheduled at distances in the future to check things out. Over the succeeding ten years she has functioned well without further therapy. My only contact with her, except for the writing of this book, has been to see her twice when crises occurred in the lives of her children. In her writings, prepared for this sharing of her story, Sarina said these words about our work together:

You were unique in my experience with counselors (I know you're not asking for this; it is a fact). Your attitude was one of deep acceptance. And it was more than unbiased acceptance, it was warm acceptance. In comparison Dr. Cioffi's was a kind of cool, impartial, scientific acceptance. (Maybe this is overstated a bit.) Your attitude toward me was personal.

Sarina's search for personal growth and meaning has gone on apace since I last saw her. Her children are now successfully on their own (they were of junior high and high school age when we worked together), and Sarina has made some profound changes in her life-style. Some years ago she became interested in "peace" issues and has since been involved in demonstrations against nuclear weapons, tracking the transport of hazardous waste products, and helping refugees from oppressed Central American countries. She has been living in "Koinonia"-type Christian communities where personal possessions are minimal and the literal teachings of Jesus are taken seriously and form the ethical framework for relationships. Sarina seems to be happier in this setting than at any time while I have known her. She has expressed some of her feelings about this in a recent circular letter to "Family and Friends":

My only experiences in intentional Christian community are here at X for the last ten months and at Y where I spent sixteen days over Christmas break. . . . Everyone in both of these communities is committed to trying to follow Jesus' teachings. I find that living with others who are consciously trying to live as Christians makes for a very caring and supportive environment. I have found everyone in both of these communities to be amazingly patient and accepting of each other. People have a deep respect for each other.

The letter goes on to describe the simple life-style, shared labor, limited funds, and warm relationships that have become part of Sarina's way of life. She seems to have taken an implicit vow of poverty in exchange for clear ideals, warm relationships, and increased self-esteem. There is no despair evident in the tone of her voice on the phone, her letters to family and friends, or in the material she so generously prepared for my use here. She laughs freely and often now.

Conclusions and Summary

In this chapter I have shared the poignant stories of three human beings who drank deeply from the cup of despair;

they nearly died, but came back to live more fully. These stories recorded the facts as accurately as time, and the need to protect the identity of the storytellers, would allow, and offer insight into the conditions that create suffering in the lives of "ordinary people." Fortunately for us, these persons had gifts of intelligence, insight, and memory that have opened windows into the causes of despair, the nature of despair, and some of the ways in which recovery from despair takes place. These "case histories" provide authenticity, depth, and insight, but they bear the limitation of all phenomenological research: They can only be applied to other cases with caution and humility. (Come to think of it, if Freud had conscientiously followed that precept, psycho-analysis might not have existed.)

I propose now to consider these narratives in the light of our earlier discussion to see in what ways we are enabled to understand these people, and their suffering, more fully. I believe the reader would agree that all three of these stories fit the summarizing definition of suffering used at the conclusion of chapter 1 and quoted above.

At the end of chapter 2, I suggested four prevenient structures that could determine the nature of suffering and the sufferer's response to it. In many ways they also appear to "fit" the data.

1. The Self-Esteem Structure

It is evident from each of the stories that a battered self-esteem lay at the core of the crisis of despair. There are really two dimensions to consider with regard to this diminished self-esteem: the developmental history and the precipitating events. What were the problems in the development of the self that made the person vulnerable to despair and what were the stresses in the precipitating situation that triggered the "crisis of despair"?

a) Sinclair was touched by childhood polio leaving him emotionally scarred and physically weakened. In addition, both his mother and brother suffered from mental illness. He learned to be distant, cautious, not too trusting. Neither his emotionally distant father, nor his emotionally troubled mother were able to provide the "holding" and "stroking" that were necessary for the optimal development of the self. For all these reasons, he did not see himself as a desirable person and had trouble accepting himself. He developed a lonely, contained life-style that provided a functional but fragile self-structure. This was only a limited base for the management of crisis, since it lacked flexibility and deep reserves of positive self-regard.

Because he had learned to survive and cope, despite these deficits in his family structure, and because he was an intelligent man with intact ego functions, Sinclair was a good candidate for consistent, structured, empathic psychotherapy. He did well on large doses of acceptance and understanding.

The ability to communicate acceptance and understanding requires more than naive kindness. It requires human experience and a background of theoretical and clinical preparation that allows responses to be specific and practical. Understanding a patient in therapy requires an understanding of the geographical, familial, valuational, and religious experiences from which the person speaks. Such generalizations as "Jewish," "Protestant," "Midwestern," "upper middle-class" are not helpful in responding with empathy to the patient's statements. Although they may help set the general situation accurately, they leave obscure the nuances that are needed for understanding. As my colleague Dick Kahn, an able psychiatrist, often pointed out in a case conference we once shared, there is nothing so useful and reassuring to the patient as gentle curiosity, a sincere interest in anything the patient wishes to tell you.

So it was that Sinclair and I worked together to repair, and in some instances to grow, his self-esteem.

b) Ted had a developmental image of himself as a dull, underachieving person who lived a life of passive, compulsive self-defeat. His father occupied a central role both in the family and in the setting of the private academies where he taught. Ted did not seem to have the "star quality" to compete with this benignly dominant figure. Instead, he deferred evaluation through passive-aggressive delaying mechanisms, always pushing deadlines, turning work in at the last minute, and performing below his potential level of competence. He got attention, but almost always in the form of pressure. In addition, he was the emotional caregiver of his mother. He showed her great courtesy and attention, but felt used and manipulated underneath. All of these circumstances conspired to cut off any real emotional warmth or unqualified affirmation from his parents.

c) Sarina learned to believe early in her life that women had fewer rights than men, had more limited futures, and got stuck with more unpleasant tasks. She thought that women who were attracted to other women were especially reprehensible in the culture in which she lived. For all these reasons, and despite significant academic and personal accomplishments, she saw herself as an undesirable person. In addition to this, she had always had a prickly relationship with her mother, who, although she was reliable as a housekeeper, cook, and organizer, was emotionally rigid and ungiving. Her academic achievements and constraints on impulse behavior were simply expected of her. Being a "good person" meant conforming and was expected, instead of being rewarded. There were precious few positive strokes, and these were given for role conformity rather than personal qualities.

"Unconditional positive regard" feels good but may be too unspecific to help the person in therapy move to the next levels of self-understanding and self-acceptance.[5] I believe it is this combination of experience, training, and theory that caused Sarina to experience my work with her as being more understanding and more "personal" than had been the case with other therapists. The structures of the professional relationship were not different, the therapeutic procedure may not have been different, but the sense of being accepted and understood was.

d) In all three cases there were problems in common. These included problems in sexual identity that interfered with mutuality, closeness, and the free expression of libido. Ted saw himself as being an impotent and undesirable person and thus had difficulty attaching positive and gratifying affect to sexual activity. He had a solitary, narcissistic, fantasied sexual life that led him to remain single until he married his brother's widow. When he felt reasonably good about himself, or was in a loving romantic relationship, he performed well, but this soon broke down when conditions were less ideal.

Because of his negative view of himself and his uncertainty about his sexual identity, Sinclair felt safer sexually with men but also fantasized sexual relationships with women. In the main, his sexuality had never been channeled into interpersonal activities. Most of the time he was celibate.

Sarina's developmental problems around sexual identity, and their consequent effect on her self-esteem, have been rather thoroughly discussed above.

e) As a result of their developmentally damaged self-images all three of these persons were vulnerable to sudden and traumatic blows to self-esteem. Each had a different set of precipitating crises for the despair in which I found them. In Ted's case it was the death of his brother, eventually followed by the break-up of his marriage. It was simply too much for his beleaguered self-esteem. He turned his rage on himself and almost achieved his own destruction. In Sarina's case it was the war between her role as "the good wife" and her secret longings to be physically united to loving women. Her husband's infidelity increased her need for succor making her more vulnerable to her lesbian wishes. The separation and divorce, which left her emotionally stranded with the care of her children, was the *coup de grâce* to her self-esteem. Her inability to manage all these insoluble problems plunged her into a depression that had powerful suicidal potential. And of course, Sinclair's self-image took a nosedive when he was stricken with Guillain-Barré syndrome. This new blow to his already shaky body image was a nearly fatal blow to his self-esteem.

f) The tasks of therapy with each of them were: to support the person through the crisis, reducing anxiety through the use of pragmatic considerations like scheduling, next-step planning, and strategies for dealing with the difficult situations in their lives; to help them bear the "bad news" of their despairing situations without trying to apply "magical" solutions to their problems; to provide a consistent supporting relationship without allowing it to become a magical countertransference; to recognize and reflect the positive qualities in each person through respect and attention rather than through words of approval; to help them sort through their values and understandings of their world as they attempted to find new meaning in an altered life situation; to believe at all times that they had it in them to overcome their despair and that they, rather than the therapist, would know what was best for them in the long run.

These tactics surely helped in the reclamation of self-esteem, but the drive toward self-actualization or the teleological pull toward higher levels of being was the motor that drove the process. Physicians, psychotherapists, counselors, nurses, and clergy all function more effectively if they learn and practice their specialties well, but they must not confuse their competence with the patient's drive toward wholeness, the human being's ability to heal himself or herself. This drive is part of the Nature of things.

2. The Self-Protective Structure

I suppose every human being has a self-protective structure. In using this term I am referring to something more akin to Becker's "vital lie"[6] than to Anna Freud's mechanisms of defense.[7] Becker takes the position that life's possibilities, like the magnitude of the universe, are overwhelming. Because of the fear of being overwhelmed,

Man had to invent and create out of himself the limitations of perception and the equanimity to live on this planet. And so the core of psychodynamics, the formation of the human character, is a study in human self-limitation. The hostility to psychoanalysis in the past, today, and in the future, will always be a hostility against admitting that man lives by lying to himself about himself and about his world, and that character, to follow Ferenczi and Brown, is a vital lie. I particularly like the way Maslow has summed up this contribution of Freudian thought:

"Freud's greatest discovery, the one which lies at the root of psychodynamics, is that *the* great cause of much psychological illness is the fear of knowledge of oneself—of one's emotions, impulses, memories, capacities, potentialities, of one's destiny. We have discovered that fear of knowledge of oneself is often isomorphic with, parallel with, fear of the outside world. . . .

"In general this kind of fear is defensive, in the sense that it is a protection of our self-esteem, of our love and respect for ourselves."[8]

I think of the self-protective structure not so much in the sense of specific defensive maneuvers such as intellectualization, rationalization, reaction formations, splitting and so on; nor as a delusional system or a psychotic pseudo-community (although given enough genetic predisposition and situational stress it might come to that), but as a tent that one builds over and around oneself to reduce the cosmic perimeters within which one lives. The inside of that tent can then be painted with projections, illusions, explanations, and relationships that limit the world and make it explainable to oneself. The tent is data and experience limited. Experience that lies outside the tent is not symbolized, explained, or incorporated. A certain myopia may develop that will not even allow the inhabitant of the tent to be conscious of such experience. The tent dweller tends to bring into the tent only those persons who are willing to share its assumptions and limits. These tents may contain few or many inhabitants. For example, members of cultist religions live within such a tent. Although the tent may have slightly different perimeters for various members of the cult, its general dimensions are clearly known and shared. Keeping the tent intact is so crucial that persons who try to expand its limits may be excommunicated, exorcised, or even killed. Individual "neurotic" systems are examples of such a tent. The reader may recall the powerful and sensitive Woody Allen movie *Interiors* wherein the entire family was profoundly affected by the mother's tightly controlled obsessional-delusional system. As in all cases where there is a self-protective tent erected, painful decisions about whether those who loved her would be "in" or "out" of the tent, or which "reality" one would believe and align with, absorbed enormous human energy. The same painful decision constantly faces those who live with paranoid loved ones, educated children of fundamentalist parents, homosexual persons living in a straight culture, and many others.

Becker's point in speaking of the "vital lie" however, was not that one must be cultist, obsessional, paranoid, or neurotic to develop such a system. He believed that it was indigenous to being human; that one must protect oneself from the twin terrors of being human: (a) being overwhelmed by the possibilities of life, and (b) being threatened with nonbeing. I suppose that when one thinks of these self-protective systems of limiting, explaining, and maintaining one's world, they seem less crazy as they become more broadly shared, that is, more consensual. (The consensual craziness shared in Nazi Germany is an example *ad absurdum* of this point.) Even our understandings of nature are consensually interpreted. The shift from metaphysics to epistemology, from material to relational explanations of the universe is an example of a shifting consensus. The broader and more stable the consensus, and the more it relates to our own experience, the more "real" things seem to be. Or to put it psychologically, the better our grip on "reality."

I believe also that it is normal for the dimensions of this tent to be enlarged as one grows. Both education and psychotherapy are methods by which one's self-protective structure grows, changes, and includes more of "reality"; each of them is intended to put holes in the roof of the tent, affording glimpses of what lies beyond. This is also true of other experiences such as travel and conversation. As one matures, the dimensions of the tent enlarge over and over again; but the insides of the tent become more specifically explicated at the same time. To the degree that one is free to experience emotions, the inside of the tent becomes more colorful.

In the case of our three friends, Sinclair, Ted, and Sarina, there were clear limits on relationships, impulse expression, ambitions, and creativity. At the height (or depth) of the crisis, all had pulled the tent in around themselves. They could hardly imagine life outside the reduced confines of their own suffering. Each made a negative projection upon the immediate world. Sarina and Ted focused with rageful intensity on expartners whom they saw as having caused so much pain. Sinclair saw the world as untrustworthy and dangerous. In each case there was a narcissistic turning inward that is common to many sufferers. Options were diminished, problems harder to solve, support systems reduced.

Sometimes persons in such circumstances turn to doctrinaire cultist systems as a way to diminish the danger of the outside world, accepting and using these systems of conditioning to maintain the reduced limits of the tent. Fortunately, all three of our friends were too wise and too determined to take such a course. And fortunately, each was able to maintain an intact ego structure without resorting to bizarre delusional systems or other evidences of more severe mental illness.

3. The Ultimate Context Structure

All three of our recovered sufferers valued life. In the depth of their despair, they had images of human closeness, a potentially more benign world, and at least the idea of a loving God.

Ted seemed to feel something like this: I know the world is orderly and God is good, so why am I so miserable? I must be a terrible failure. Maybe even God cannot love me. Although he blamed and hated God for the failure of his marriage, it seemed to be a temporary alienation. The measure of the recovery of his relationship with God was exemplified by the fact that his second wedding took place as part of a Sunday morning church service. It was widely attended and was a time of joy shared by many members of the community. Ted was very serious about the sacramental quality of this service. It was obvious that he took his promises to God and to his bride seriously, from a religious point of view. It may be too much to say that Ted now has a more positive cosmic view. Whether the world has changed for him I cannot say, but he has changed. He is more confident. He exercises more power over his own destiny and seems to have made peace with the ultimate beliefs with which he entered into his deepest suffering.

Sarina has recovered the power of some of her deepest religious feelings. Although she is more deeply spiritual, she is also more disillusioned with organized religion. After all, her husband, who cheated on her, and two of the therapists who seemed to misunderstand and reject her growing lesbian identity, were clergypersons. In her recent letter reviewing the history of her illness and recovery, she had some very specific things to say about this:

All I want to say here is, if I ever needed counseling again or if I were in the position of making a recommendation to someone who did, I would not go to a pastoral counselor who was working within the institutional church, because I believe such counselors are likely to share the church's attitude toward homosexuality. I would be glad to consider or recommend a pastoral counselor who worked outside the context of the church. (I don't mean the building.) This attitude on my part may be strengthened by the fact that I have also given up on the institutional church when it comes to doing anything significant on peace and justice issues.

As one who has trained several "brands" of therapists there is in me a gentle rejoinder to Sarina. All prospective therapists should have an opportunity through supervision, and through their own personal therapy, to overcome homophobia or any other tendency to reject persons because of their values or life-styles. Therapists, like anyone else, have the right to their own religious and social values, but the successful practice of psychotherapy requires that they be able to move beyond differences in values and life-style in the interest of acceptance and empathy, or be wise enough to refer clients to a more appropriate therapist.

So Sarina is deeply committed to the core of Christian values, that is, to teachings of Jesus, but both as a lesbian and as an active peace advocate she has lost faith in the institutional church as a spiritual home for herself. She may be speaking for many other persons with these same identities. Sarina's wish to make a difference in the world in which she lives has shifted to actively opposing atomic weaponry and actively succoring victims of political oppression. In order to live out these values she has become willing to give up financial security and all the materialistic evidences of success. These attitudes do indeed seem congruent with the teachings of Jesus. From her own perspective I am sure that Sarina would feel that her ultimate context has been changed and strengthened by what she has learned as a direct result of her suffering.

Sinclair has expanded the frame of his life to include community involvement, reading Francis of Assisi, keeping up vigorous correspondence with his friends, and thinking about ultimate and spiritual topics. The cynicism that has stood him in such good stead by fending off disappointment and keeping him from expecting too much from life, still holds steady. But there is a gentle contemplative edge to Sinclair's often caustic observations.

When I consider the ultimate structures of Sinclair and Sarina, which include strong unconventional religious ideation, I am reminded of the words of Victor Frankl. In discussing what he called "uniquely human phenomena," he wrote:

There is one which I regard as the most representative of the human reality. I have circumscribed this phenomenon in terms of "man's [and woman's] search for meaning." Now if this is correct, one may also be justified in defining religion as man's [and woman's] search for *ultimate* meaning. It was Albert Einstein who once contended that to be religious is to have found an answer to the question, What is the meaning of life? If we subscribe to this statement we may then define belief and faith as trust in ultimate meaning. . . .

The concept of religion in its widest possible sense, as it is here espoused, certainly goes far beyond the narrow concepts of God promulgated by many representatives of denominational and institutional religion. They often depict, not to say denigrate, God as a being who is primarily concerned with being believed in, by the greatest possible number of believers, and along the lines of a specific creed, at that. "Just believe," we are told, "and everything will be okay." But alas, not only is this order based on a distortion of any sound concept of deity, but even more important, it is doomed to failure: obviously, there are certain activities that simply cannot be commanded, demanded, or ordered, and as it happens, the triad "faith, hope and love" belongs to this class of activities that elude an approach with, so to speak, "command characteristics."[9]

Sarina and Sinclair have learned that shibboleths and cliches are of little value; in the long run it is actions that count. They are not hooked on the idea of a narcissistic God offering cheap grace in exchange for obsessional affirmations. All three of the friends who have shared this chapter with us have sought to understand their lives more fully. They have attempted to see their lives in the light of ultimate meaning and are healthier and richer for having done so.

4. The Human Support Structure

For all of our three sufferers, the key to healing lay in the human support system. Whether one looks at the problem of suffering from a physical, psychological, or spiritual point of view, the instruments of peace and healing are human beings. Sarina, Ted, and Sinclair all had limited, but deep and enduring, friendships before the suffering reached crisis proportions. Sarina had one couple and one older woman who were very constant and trustworthy in offering acceptance and support. Her sister was very caring. At a point where she felt overwhelmed with child-care, she was able to send her daughter to live with her sister for a school semester. As she began to feel more in control of her situation, she reached out to a women's support group, which was of great help to her. In common with Sinclair and Ted, she knew how to ask for help.

Sinclair also had a few close relationships. Two of the most stalwart were a gay couple who were extremely caring during the severest stages of Sinclair's illness. They visited him in the hospital and made themselves available for shopping, cooking, and other forms of sustenance care when he was able to come home. As we worked together, I grew to appreciate the support network for persons with handicapping conditions that existed with the State and Federal government. Rehabilitative equipment was supplied, including special equipment for an automobile. Rehabilitation therapists and social workers made regular visits to Sinclair to see that his physical needs were met. He was shuttled back and forth to medical appointments and received many other demonstrations of human concern.

At the point where Sinclair was able to matriculate for his second master's degree, the academic institution to which he applied was flexible and considerate, adjusting hours and reducing course load so that Sinclair could manage this very difficult task. I'm sure that he would agree that there were a surprising number of kind persons in his world.

Ted was in many ways the most urbane and community involved of the three sufferers. His role as a middle school teacher, a church member, and an officer in his college alumni association gave him a wide range of contacts. But the core of his friendships was limited to three or four persons. He too experienced much caring outreach, during the periods before and after his suicide attempt. It was my impression that people cared for him more than he could let himself know that they did. Still, Ted has suffered at the hands of the community. Rough middle school boys have accused him of being "a fag" even though he is not. He had also a strong, but ambivalent relationship with his mother, who was more narcissistic than nurturant, but who never abandoned him during his travail. Ted was also able to ask for help. The human support network, including psychotherapy, was vital in his recovery from despair.

Recently, as an unexpected gift, I received a few pages of delightful doggerel written by Sinclair during October and November of 1988. The piece that follows is an appropriate reminder that no matter how clever our analyses of and insights into other persons may be, the business of psychotherapy deals with metaphors and images that are but fleeting glimpses of the "other's" reality.

Mirror Image

What I see,
is not,
What you see,
in me.

142

OVERCOMING DESPAIR

I am reversed to you,
as you are reversed to me.
ECNALUBMA IS AMBULANCE
when mirrored and rear-viewed.

I try to wonder,
and often wander,
through the looking glass,
to see you as you see me.

I exist as image,
to myself.
But is myself more real to thyself,
than thee to me??

Such a sense of richness comes to me as I think about the years I spent with Sarina, Sinclair, and Ted. How poignantly they shared their pain; with what herculean effort they emerged from the "slough of despond";[10] what a vital contribution they are making to the world as recoverers from despair; what hope their recovery provides for all the rest of us sufferers. The ingredients for their recovery are clear: a few good friends, a desire for life, a willingness to pay the price for growth, knowing how to ask for help, the gift of modern medical technology, acceptance, empathy, and the unseen Telos that pulls us all to new and greater levels of existence. With only the tiniest bit of imagination, I hear your voices joining mine as I raise three cheers for Sinclair, Ted, and Sarina.

CHAPTER FIVE

Responding to the Sufferer

The Universal Nature of Suffering

In chapter 1 we introduced the tragic figure of Tom, who, beset by a world of imagined attackers, suffered the tortures of the damned in a world peopled by his febrile imagination. In the same chapter we focused on the figure of Job, who was a boil-covered, pus-ridden catastrophe, sitting in the midst of a plethora of physical problems. Then we introduced the intense middle-age depression of Tolstoy, who shared his suffering in such powerful, poignant prose that we were drawn into the experience with him.

Since then we have met several compelling characters: the professor and his wife, Aunt Betty, Sinclair, Ted, Sarina, and others. The causes of the suffering of these figures ranged from the almost purely physical to the almost entirely psychological. Looking across these carefully chosen examples of suffering, and extending our purview to experiences of our own, and to those to whom we have given care, we are forced into certain conclusions.

1. We all must face losses. We all face or have faced the death of our parents. Many of us will eventually face the deaths of our brothers, sisters, children, and beloved friends. When loved ones die the numbing loss attacks the unity of our world and threatens our self-esteem. We also face our

own deaths. Whether we have much or little time to prepare, whether death's appearance is gentle or violent, it brings impending losses. We face the end of friendships, dreams, and responsibilities that we hold dear. Every separation is a mini-death and every loss is a dress rehearsal for our own departure. So we are involved in either anticipatory grief or conventional grief, one from the aura of impending loss and the other from the tragedy of separation.[1]

Death is not the only loss that can cause suffering. Losing our marriages, businesses, friendships, and health all have their own heavy emotional toll.

2. We all must face pain. Almost all of us have experienced, or will experience, traumatic or debilitating illness. Despite the great medical progress in diminishing the discomfort in terminal illness, we will all experience pain before our lives are over. There will be enormous differences in the intensity, disorganization, and psychological discomfort that we experience, but pain awaits most of us. In many cases this pain will become a trigger for suffering.

3. Suffering is equally authentic whether it is caused by normal or pathological events. The "reality" of suffering is not determined by whether the experiences leading to the suffering are "pathological" or "normal." It is evident from our earlier discussion that Tom's pain may have been just as great as Job's pain, that Tolstoy's pain may have been just as great as that of the professor and his wife. It is not the source that determines the nature or intensity of suffering. However, because it defies modern understandings of meaningfulness, "pathological" suffering may be harder to accept, understand, and alleviate through treatment.

4. Pain and loss reach beyond themselves in activating latent problems in emotional balance, self-esteem, and cosmic comfort. Events such as health crises, the loss of family members, loss of employment, and national and social catastrophes may serve to penetrate the "vital lie" of our lives, acting as windows to deep levels of existential terror against which we have heretofore successfully defended. Such events point out that meaning in our lives requires a sense of cosmic

certainty (of faith) that is essentially spiritual in nature. When such events open windows of uncertainty we suffer.

5. Events that cause suffering in the short term may have long-term positive effects. Existential crises that are occasions for suffering are also opportunities for change. Such events provide windows into one's world view, human relations, and understandings of oneself. These openings allow positive changes in attitudes, relationships, and values to take place. After a period of suffering there may be a transformation in one's priorities. I once wrote about such a transformation:

The greatest value of Barbara's death for me as her father was the stripping away of the "vital lie." The lie of role importance as a substitute for personhood, the lie of elaborate theological rational-izations as a defense against my need for God and my helplessness before [God]. There came to me afresh things that I had dimly known to be true—the importance of rest, beauty, and health. I work at home now in my study-office, reading, writing, training therapists, doing psychotherapy . . . looking out the windows at the mountains. Now I know I will never be as great as I was driven to be but better perhaps than I thought I could be.[2]

Periods of suffering may create changes in eating habits, exercise, and leisure that can enrich and prolong life. Many persons trace the greatest experiences of personal growth and insight to periods of suffering.

We Are All Sufferers Together

It is my position here that we are all sufferers together; we simply take turns being sufferers and caregivers. During the polio epidemic of 1955–56, a doctor, courageously treating persons who were battling that terrible disease, occasionally became infected. There ensued the heartbreaking picture of the caregiver joining the sufferers in the most literal way possible.

Looking beyond the personal tragedy of the caregiver become sufferer, one sees an important metaphor. It is a metaphor that reflects theological doctrines of incarnation, including the central Christian myth, where the god-man assumes pain and suffering, even death, for those he loves. The metaphor reflects the shifting incarnations of Hindu mythology as well. As the beautiful boy is supposed to have said in anthropologist Heinrich Zimmer's account of the myth of Indra: "Life in the cycle of the countless rebirths is like a vision in a dream. The gods on high, the mute trees and the stones, are like apparitions in this phantasy. But Death administers the law of time. Ordained by time, Death is the master of all. . . . In unending cycles the good and evil alternate."[3]

Or, for our purposes, the caregiver and the sufferer alternate. As he neared his death my father expressed the transitions in his own life cycle in the simplest of terms: "You come into the world a child and you go out of the world a child." This potential return to childhood, to dependency, is an important thing to remember during one's salad days of independence, success, and prosperity. The physician contracting polio in his or her most heroic moment is an example of one human being giving all for the healing of another. But it is also a sober reminder that expertise and status are often exchanged for illness and dependency. The denial of the caregiver's own mortality can result in procedural carelessness leading to infection, illness, even death.

We are taught in theology that our value as human beings is intrinsic, that it is a gift of God not dependent on our own works. But caregivers have learned that it is important to our self-esteem for us to be of service to one another while we can do so. For ultimately we are to be sufferers together.

Suffering Is a Gift

Suffering is a gift that helps caregivers. When we treat others, we recognize pain because we have it ourselves. It is against the tapestry of our own pain that we understand the suffering of others. When we sit with the dying we have a sense of the territory because we recognize that we are looking at our own future. When we hear a sufferer's tragic story we respond with empathy because we reach within ourselves for emotions that resonate with the story we are being told. Medical practitioners are made gentler in their treatment of others by the memory of their own pain. Within limits, suffering enables empathy.

Suffering is not an abstraction; it is a personal reality. It opens windows in our lives to deep currents of personal pain that have been flowing silently for years. It is at such times that existential, relational, and ultimate questions are triggered which have remained dormant within us during normal circumstances. It is at such times that we may discover that suffering provides a special opportunity for a deeper look at our relationships, beliefs, behaviors, and particularly, our values.

Compulsivity, Intentionality, and Transcendence in Suffering

Suffering has a strangely compelling effect on both sufferers and caregivers. It tends to become the focus of life's arrangements. For the sufferer, managing the simple survival tasks of life may require much energy and intricate planning. Life can become built around medications, chemotherapy sessions, changes of bandages, dialysis machines, or visits to psychotherapists. It can also become built around periods of painful obsessions and fantasies. There may be little "conflict free" energy left to be used for creative purposes.[4] To remain creatively involved in the face of suffering requires great intentionality. Suffering can be like a vortex that sucks both sufferers and caregivers into its vacuous center. Suffering, with its often unrewarding, repetitive demands, pushes both sufferer and caregiver toward stereotyped behaviors.

Tillich has written that the vitality of human life lies in its intentionality: "Vitality, power of life, is correlated to the kind of life to which it gives power. The power of a man's [or woman's] life cannot be seen separately from what the medieval philosophers called 'intentionality,' the relation to meanings."[5]

One of the great dangers of suffering is the potential loss of intentionality. One stops making plans; one gives up being in control; one yields to the compulsive routines of suffering. This is true not only of the sufferer, but also of those who provide care. Whether one speaks of machines or human activity, repetition tends to reduce meaning. In order to remain intentional in the face of pain, one must see beyond it. For the sufferer, the more chronic and permanent the condition, the greater the likelihood that meaning will be lost. For the caregiver, the more routine and impersonal the caregiving role, the more meaningless it is apt to become.

If creativity, vitality, and meaning are to be maintained in the face of suffering, responses must be not only intentional, but also transcendent. In order for transcendence to happen in the face of suffering, one must have the courage not only to be, but also to become. This brings us to what I consider the "primary" roles of the caregiver or, preferably, the caregiving team.

1. To be with the sufferer. As caregivers, if we can do nothing else, we can be with the sufferer. This is the essential qualification for successful caring: the ability to be present. Being is both more fundamental to caring, and more difficult, than doing.

2. To minister to the sufferer's needs. This more active side of caregiving includes a wide range of responses including medical and surgical procedures, nursing care, feeding and cleaning, education, priestly activities, and communications (with family, friends, businesses, etc.)

3. To be aware of the sufferer's ultimate context. That is, to help provide a more extended and relational context for the sufferer. For the sufferer, being gripped by a spasm of pain is similar in quality to being caught in a panic anxiety attack; the experience is totally absorbing. It is not a time for seeing visions, dreaming dreams, or looking to the future; it is a time to hang on for dear life. It is the caregiver's responsibility not only to be present during the sufferer's pain and to minister to the sufferer's needs but also to maintain a contextual perspective for the sufferer.

Ministering to the sufferer's needs is a demanding and absorbing survival necessity. Being present with the sufferer

149

in his or her pain, apprehension, and despair is a recognition that suffering, no matter how personal, occurs in an interpersonal setting. Being aware of the sufferer's ultimate context recognizes that human beings reach beyond the limits of their organisms into intricate interpersonal, intellectual, and spiritual dimensions. It is by focusing on elements of the sufferer's context beyond the pain, the physical care, the daily housekeeping and business concerns that the sufferer may be helped to resume meaningful interpersonal, intellectual, and spiritual activities, thus transcending the limits of despair.

Being able to maintain perspective takes the caregiver one step beyond the vortex of suffering. Being able to provide a relationship that reaches the sufferer's distress, is another step. But being able to see enhanced meaning and deepened growth as a distinct possibility in suffering is a giant step. Before we discuss these ideas further, let us turn to some practical problems that face the caregiver.

Understanding the Sufferer's Style

Most persons do not have a stereotyped response to suffering. Nuances of response may be as varied as are human beings. Because of this very complexity we tend to impose conventions on complex data in order to understand them better. If we realize that these are clusters of descriptive ideas, rather than morphic entities, such conventions can often be helpful. Therefore I will risk using four principal "types" of response to suffering. I believe that these types will seem familiar to experienced caregivers. I will order them on an implicit value continuum from least to most adaptive.

1. Surrender and Withdrawal

The most profound example of withdrawal is suicide. Whether or not it is an act of surrender or unyielding rage depends on the person. But in terms of social psychologist Kurt Lewin's conflict model it certainly means leaving the field.[6] This response is particularly hard on caregivers, to say nothing of the families of suicide victims, since it permanently interrupts the relationship, often leaving behind a mélange of feelings of sorrow, guilt, and failure. There has been a tendency among professional caregivers to label suicidal behavior as emotionally disturbed, even "psychotic," no matter how compelling the life circumstances may be.

I believe that suicide as a solution to unbearable circumstances may run across the entire range of wellness and pathology. When I am tempted to believe that only mentally disturbed persons commit suicide, I always remember a parishioner whom I shall call Grandpa Woodling. Grandpa Woodling was in his eighties, long since retired. He lived by himself in a converted summer cottage near a beautiful lake. He was not isolated, having concerned neighbors around him. He was widely loved and appreciated by the community in which he lived. But one winter day Grandpa Woodling took his shotgun, went to the outhouse, held the muzzle to his stomach, and shot himself. As you might imagine, it was difficult for me, a young pastor, to explain to myself and his friends what had happened.

I never knew what caused Grandpa Woodling to take his own life. He may have had bad news from his doctor. He may have decided that life was no longer worth the daily struggle. But of one thing I feel sure: By any conventional psychological measurements, he was sane.

Fortunately, most sufferers signal increasing despair before attempting suicide, and in most cases proper psychiatric and spiritual care will tide them over the self-destructive crisis. But caregivers of severely depressed or intensely suffering persons should prepare themselves to deal with this ultimate withdrawal.

Other Forms of Surrender

Some persons simply surrender themselves to the mechanics of suffering. They narrow their frames of reference to reject potentially vital, contemporary life events. Often they lose interest in the activities of other persons. There is almost a return to "primary narcissism."[7]

Often such persons develop a litany that may take one of three forms: It may consist of complaints about the injustices of life, stressing their own unimportance and the perception that no one cares about their existence (particularly such key figures as spouses, children, or clergy). It may take the form of an endless recitation of the medical bulletin of the day. This may include medications, bowel movements, and endless intimate, detailing of physiological minutiae. Finally, it may take the form of memorializing the past. In this case, a ritual is devised wherein past relationships, triumphs, and occupations are remembered and embellished while present possibilities are ignored. All of these are attempts to derive a "cosmic specialness" from a negative present state of affairs. Such efforts not only obviate the need to become involved in changing one's situation, but may also provide a rationale for withdrawal.

There are several aspects of this approach that make it difficult for caregivers. First, it tends to defeat empathy. A caregiver can only resonate to a self-defeating ritual for a limited period of time without become bored or disgusted. When this happens, responses to the sufferer become superficial and a subtle disrespect may creep in. Second, many caregivers are easily seduced by dependency. Their responses may range from unconsciously underwriting regression, by treating sufferers as children, to "managing" them. There is a danger that caregivers will over respond to the "needy" qualities in such sufferers, implicitly promising more nurture than they can sustain, then ultimately reject the sufferer. A kindly, ego-supportive approach is often useful, supporting the sufferer's ability to take care of himself or herself. In any difficult relationship there must be limits. These should be stated forthrightly and only changed by mutual negotiation. It is often possible to provide activity that will shift the narcissistic focus away from the sufferer's "rituals" for increasing periods of time.

It is important in such cases to be able to separate grief from chronic depression. In such cases a team approach to caring, with multiple skills and good communication between team members, is most helpful. Medical, psychological, rehabilitative, and clergy persons working together can respond to physical, psychological, and spiritual needs. Working as a team will allow professional personnel to devise appropriate tactics for helping the sufferer to both heal and grow.

When it is physically possible for the patient to be part of a support group, this can be very helpful. Groups tend to elicit feelings, symbolize shared experiences, and present no-nonsense responses to self-pitying and defeatist behaviors.

2. COUNTERDEPENDENCY AND AGGRESSION

In dealing with suffering, anger is often better than sadness and assertiveness better than compliance. Persons who are willing to fight for themselves probably have a better chance of survival. Many persons suffering from physical illness mobilize enough energy to become crotchety, reactive, or even hostile. Since they feel miserable anyway, they simply "ride the camel in the direction it's going."[8] Such counter-dependency, although it is usually more mobilizing to the personality than surrender or despair, alienates other persons, tending to keep them at a distance. This behavior is often a self-fulfilling prophecy; it is easy to prove that people do not "really" care, if we make them uncomfortable enough. They will simply stay away. I have often found that subtle humor, offered as paradoxical intention, can serve as a helpful riposte to this particular style of suffering. Besides, like a porcupine's quills, such reactive behavior generally covers a soft center.

Sometimes the energy in this approach can be turned into redemptive effort. Mwalimu Imara tells the story of just such a patient: "I was told that the patient, Miss Martin, was recovering from rather extensive abdominal surgery for cancer, and the more she healed the more demanding, abusive, foul mouthed and cantankerous she became. The chaplain's office was called in as a last-ditch effort to sweeten her up a little for the staff's sake until she was well enough to be sent to a nursing home."[9]

Through the patient daily ministry of pastoral care, this

patient's story unfolded. She had been competent, successful, and increasingly lonely throughout her lifetime. When her serious (ultimately terminal) illness was discovered, she responded with incredible bitterness. But through careful spiritual direction and group work she was transformed into a woman who said to her group, "I have lived more in the past three months than I have during my whole life." Just like any major change in life, serious illness, with all its suffering, is an opportunity to evaluate, reconsider, and start in a new direction.

This poignant story points out an important principle for caregivers to remember. That is, that growth can continue until the hour of death. If we accept each great sorrow as a challenge to understanding human existence more deeply, then death becomes another opportunity for growth. In the case of Miss Martin, there were the facilities and personnel for a positive team approach to her problem: (1) The medical personnel recognized a spiritual problem when they saw it; (2) a skilled chaplain took the time to hear all of her story; (3) groups were available with which she could interact for support and appropriate confrontation; and (4) the Spirit of God (or the principle of self-actualization) provided the energy for change, even in the face of impending death.

3. MASTERING PAIN AND STAYING IN TOUCH

Those who have suffered severe physical pain may feel that it cannot really be mastered, only modified and controlled. However, it is often possible to move pain from the center of one's perceptual focus to the periphery, focusing on the world beyond one's pain, so that interest in relationships, ideas, and future plans can continue. As we noted in chapter 3, great progress is being made in the understanding and control of physical pain. Here, however, I have broadened the meaning to include "emotional" pain as well.

I have developed a heroic fantasy, for myself, as I have thought of the suffering that surely awaits me in the future: "Bear as much as you can, use medication when you must, be as active as possible, stay in touch with your friends, and believe in the ultimate goodness of God." Knowing what Robert Burns said about the plans of mice and men, this still seems to me to be a reasonable goal. There are plenty of heroic figures to serve as examples, and proof, that such a stance, with regard to suffering, can be accomplished. I have already detailed the inspiring approaches to suffering accomplished by Sigmund Freud and my own Aunt Betty.

Such an approach to suffering requires an intact ego and considerable courage. It also requires involvement with the world and human relationships. Such a sufferer's activity focus may be on unfinished work, money management, friendships that require correspondence (cards, letters, or phone calls), journals to be written, spiritual exercises, and more. All of these are good reasons to stay alive, as are blue skies, golden sunsets, and green plants.

Sufferers are not simply haunted by physical pain; sometimes they are haunted by the limitations of old age—the painful loss of energy, colleagues, sexual vitality, employment, and interpersonal acuity.

If we are to live in a "mastering" mode during our suffering, the "road map" looks something like this:

1. Get the pain under control. One should be open to good medical care, psychotherapy, support groups, or whatever helps most.

2. Remain as involved and active as possible, particularly with regard to relationships. One should not be reluctant to share "real" feelings.

3. Plan for the future; whatever hours, days, weeks, or years are left are a golden gift.

Caregivers can help greatly by being interested in the intellectual life of the sufferer. One should remember that sufferers are persons of worth and accomplishment who have much to teach and tell. Although there are limits on the care-giver's "free" time, learning from sufferers is not time wasted.

4. Acceptance and Faith

All of us who have worked in pastoral care have at least one person etched in our memories who simply worked through and rose above suffering. Every experienced nurse or physician has worked with one or more persons who demonstrated transcendent courage in the face of severe suffering or death. Such persons are uniquely at peace, uniquely open to others, and uniquely honest. My own history is dotted with persons, seriously ill, whom I looked forward to seeing. Their unflinching honesty about their situations relieved me of the need for subterfuge; their courage provided a model for the handling of pain and suffering; and their faith in the future, even beyond this life, helped place the human struggle in an ultimate context.

Readers of the Kübler-Ross books are aware of the five stages of "growth" after one learns of one's own impending death. These are denial, anger, bargaining, preparatory depression, and acceptance. Imara wrote:

Is it so hard to think of a dying patient as having a direction, as having a life plan? Moving and living our days with a sense of coherence is the dividend that the terminally ill patient receives for moving through the five stages. The stage of acceptance, the final stage in the transcendence of the patient is the time when the person's life becomes recentered and more self sufficient.[10]

A person need not be involved in a terminal illness to learn to accept the reality of suffering, work out the meaning of life in this new and painful situation, recast the sense of time in a new and eternal framework, and begin to live more presently and fully. Suffering, a cruel and unrelenting schoolmaster, can teach us to value the present moment, while still seeing it as part of our total growth. It can help us shift our values away from competition and material success. There is often a perfection of spirit and attitude to be derived from suffering.

This does not mean, however, that it is good to suffer, per se. Suffering, by itself, does nothing but hurt. If suffering is the independent variable in our discussion, then the dependent variables are: the developmental history of the person, the prodromal ego structure and personality integration (or in Object Relations terms, the completeness of the self), the presence or absence of a satisfying faith, and the existence or nonexistence of a support community. The more of these variables that are present, and the more completely developed each of them is, the greater the likelihood that suffering will enhance humanness, grace, and maturity in the person. Suffering, like any crucible, will reveal imperfections of all kinds. Thus, if the dependent variables are lacking, suffering can leave a person brittle, fragmented, and empty. But like any crucible, suffering can also burn away the dross, leaving purity behind.

The four modes of response to suffering, presented here, are on a continuum with regard to maturity.[11] Each successive mode, from surrender and withdrawal to acceptance and faith, requires a more mature response pattern, and in turn, creates more growth. Sometimes suffering persons, like Imara's Miss Martin, move from one kind of response to another during the process of suffering. In Miss Martin's case, she took two giant steps; she moved from counterdependency and aggression to acceptance and faith.

Caring for Sufferers as a Raison d'Être

I have been convinced for some time that persons who become caregivers often view their occupations, not simply as jobs, but as a raison d'être for their entire lives. Clergypersons, pastoral counselors, and psychologists with whom I have worked have often fitted the role of "family emotional caregivers." It has seemed to me that their vocational choices went back to a childhood role of being "the one who really understood" mother or father, or the one who "kept the family together." I once did a computer search to try to uncover supportive research data for these anecdotal impressions, but there were few studies. However, I cannot shake the feeling that these hunches are accurate. To what degree these impressions reflect the vocational choices of more medically oriented caregivers, I cannot say.

If being a caregiver is a displacement of, or sublimation for, wishes to heal one's own self or family, wishes to express caring to family members, or the need to feel "especially needed" (thus deriving a sense of cosmic specialness), this may provide a powerful and problematical motivational base.

On the positive side, it provides a strong continuing flow of vocationally directed energy, arising from the personality itself. This would likely enhance staying power and an empathy with sufferers that is already indigenous to the personality. But it does have potential shortcomings.

Dangers of Overidentification with Sufferers

Overidentification is countervalent to objective evaluation, appropriate limit setting, and realistic expectations with regard to the proper rewards for caregiving. An unconscious wish to redeem one's nuclear family through caring for others or an unconscious wish to receive the rewards and appreciation that were denied in the nuclear family, will almost certainly result in feelings of being cheated and denied the deserved response for all one's caring. In addition to this, in every caring relationship, potential loss or separation is implicit in the contract. If one overidentifies with the sufferer, one may face a series of painful losses when patients die, therapy clients discontinue therapy, or, especially, when caregiving arrangements are aborted for practical or psychological reasons.

The consequences of overidentification increase the possibility of burnout. They defeat objectivity, make the setting of limits almost impossible, create feelings of loss and disappointment, and put the caregiver on an emotional roller coaster. There are two principal ways to clarify the intensity and limits of identification. The first is through professional training. All major caregiving professions have codes of ethics which help set proper limits. Supervised clinical involvement helps the person in training to come to terms with all the problems mentioned above. Second, in many cases, personal psychotherapy is a necessary adjunct to professional training, if full professional maturity is to be achieved. "Insulation" is a necessary ingredient in good professional performance. One simply cannot open up like an overripe melon every time there is a life-and-death crisis. But too much insulation defeats the entire process of caring and undercuts the sufferer's faith in his or her own ability to grow. If we are to be open enough to be empathic, without being painfully exposed to unresolved unconscious fears or wishes, considerable personal and professional maturation is needed. Despite good professional training or personal psychotherapy, the best caregiving is undertaken in company with colleagues.

If I were asked to offer a few suggestions to incipient caregivers, they might run as follows: count the cost before you enter the profession, enlist for the long haul, respect your own physiological and emotional limits, seek out and trust able mentors in your chosen field, arm yourself with facts, learn and practice the ethics of your profession, and have faith in the power of life. I close those comments with a quote from Victor Hugo: "Have courage for the great sorrows of life, and patience for the small ones. And when you have laboriously accomplished your daily task, go to sleep in peace. God is awake."[12]

For those of us who believe that the movement toward full humanness is teleological, that it is part of God's plan for us, written into Nature and our natures, caregiving is a ministry that serves as a catalyst for such growth among us and our cosufferers. It can rise above the provisions of physical survival needs, and basic needs for socialization, to offer a vision of growth and wholeness that may be achieved within the limits of the sufferer's capabilities. Suffering does not diminish basic humanness; in point of fact, it can deepen and enrich the experiences of relating and being. When such growth occurs, caregivers may unwittingly be the hand-maidens of transcendence.

CHAPTER SIX

Suffering and Meaning

Making sense of our suffering may be the most difficult and inescapable task we face. Somehow, it has to be fitted into our lives in such a way that it does not tear everything apart. If we are to be sane, we must integrate these experiences into the total picture of ourselves, and our lives, in a way that makes sense. Meaning-making is a necessary, continuing, task that becomes particularly frightening and difficult during periods of great stress.

There are an increasing number of incidents in today's society that render meaning-making exceptionally hard. While this book was being written a Pan American jet fell from the air over Scotland, smashing 249 human bodies into lifelessness. Although a moan could be heard around the world from the bereaved mothers, fathers, siblings, children, lovers, and friends of these innocent victims of terrorism, no one will ever know the suffering caused to the families of these victims by this act of terrorism.

A plastique bomb planted in the forward cargo compartment snuffed out uncountable years of human potential: art that will never be created, music that will never be written, children who will never be caressed, ideas that will never be born. In the minds of the perpetrating terrorists, there must have been some tortured rationale for destroying innocent human beings in a remote attempt to resolve a political problem. But to the living victims, the bereaved, and to the rest of the world, it was senseless. It is a shocking reminder of how little we have learned since the Holocaust.

The Holocaust, more than any other event in our life time, stretched the limits of meaning-making. The arrogant butchery of six million precious human beings, loved by God, but murdered because of their ethnic identity, staggers the imagination and defies understanding. For many it destroyed faith in reason, in justice, in order, in God. The manner in which belief died for many sufferers is epitomized in the life of Elie Wiesel, who survived after having been incarcerated in Auschwitz and Buchenwald, two of the most infamous Nazi death camps. In his book, *Night*, Wiesel recounts the events at Auschwitz, which led to the critical moment when his ability to make meaning, within the light of his faith, reached and passed its limit:

On the eve of Rosh Hashanah, the last day of that accursed year, the whole camp was electric with the tension which was in all our hearts. In spite of everything, this day was different from any other. The last day of the year. The word "last" rang very strangely. What if it were indeed the last day? . . .

Ten thousand men had come to attend the solemn service, heads of the blocks, Kapos, functionaries of death.

"Bless the Eternal. . . ."

The voice of the officiant had just made itself heard. I thought at first it was the wind.

"Blessed be the name of the Eternal!"

Thousands of voices repeated the benediction; thousands of men prostrated themselves like trees before a tempest. "Blessed be the name of the Eternal."

Why, but why should I bless Him? In every fiber I rebelled. Because He had had thousands of children burned in His pits? Because He kept six crematories working night and day, on Sundays and feast days? Because in His great might he had created Auschwitz, Birkenau, Buna, and so many factories of death? How could I say to Him: "Blessed art Thou, Eternal, Master of the Universe, who chose us from among the races to be tortured day and night, to see our fathers, our mothers, our brothers, end in the crematory? Praised be Thy Holy Name, Thou who has chosen us to be butchered on Thine altar?" . . .

Once, New Year's Day had dominated my life. I knew that my sins grieved the Eternal; I implored his forgiveness. Once, I had believed profoundly that upon one solitary deed of mine, one solitary prayer, depended the salvation of the world.

This day I had ceased to plead. I was no longer capable of lamentation. On the contrary, I felt strong. I was the accuser. God the accused. My eyes were open and I was alone—terribly alone in a world without God and without man. Without love or mercy. I had ceased to be anything but ashes, yet I felt myself to be stronger than the Almighty, to whom my life had been tied for so long. I stood amid that praying congregation, observing it like a stranger.[1]

Years later Francois Mauriac heard this story from a young Elie Wiesel himself. Wiesel came to interview him for a Tel Aviv newspaper. Mauriac had first realized the true horror of the Nazi occupation when his wife told him of a carload of Jewish children, standing outside Austerlitz station, ready to be shipped to the concentration camps. He said to Wiesel, "How often I have thought of those children," whereupon Wiesel replied, "I was one of them." In remembering his dramatic encounter with a still young Wiesel, Mauriac wrote these memorable words:

And I who believe that God is love, what answer could I give my young questioner, whose dark eyes still held the reflection of that angelic sadness which had appeared one day upon the face of the hanged child? What did I say to him? Did I speak of that other Jew, his brother, who may have resembled him—the Crucified, whose cross has conquered all the world? Did I affirm that the stumbling block to his faith, was the cornerstone of mine, and that the conformity between the Cross and the suffering of men was in my eyes the key to that impenetrable mystery whereon the faith of his childhood had perished? The Jewish nation has been resurrected from among its thousands of dead. It is through them that it lives again. We do not know the worth of one single drop of blood, one single tear. All is grace. If the Eternal is the Eternal, the last word for each one of us belongs to Him. This is what I should have told this Jewish child. But I could only embrace him, weeping.[2]

Both the necessity and the difficulty of making meaning out of suffering are evident in the painful vignettes we have quoted. Wiesel went on from that moment in which his "God" became unmasked, to become an alarum to the world. He has spent his life reminding humankind of the reality of evil and the suffering it creates. Perhaps more than any other writer, he has been determined not to let the world forget. His writings reveal that he has never forgotten the pain, but in his role of prophet, positioned between the past excesses and future sins of humankind, he has found meaning.

Mauriac's words are a determined statement of belief in belief. "If the Eternal is the Eternal, the last word for each of us, belongs to Him."[3]

This description of the Ultimate Context expresses faith in the unknown limits, the unknown ways, the unknown intentions, of the Eternal. But Mauriac did not make this statement to Wiesel; it was what he thought he should have said in retrospect. What he really did was a stronger statement; he embraced him, weeping.

Although it is clear that the life-task for all of us is to make sense of our suffering, our human struggles, it is difficult at best, and sometimes impossible to do so. That the tragedies of the Second World War were not confined to the Holocaust can be seen in the story of Brigida, who came to my office for help many years ago. Brigida has been in America only a few years when I first met her. She was a college student who came to see me for psychotherapy. She spent her early years in Germany where her father was an army officer under the Third Reich. Her mother was a professional singer. During the war she lived with her grandparents, and other relatives, in Cologne, while her father served in the war and her mother traveled, entertaining troops. As the war ground on, the city of Cologne was subject to heavy Allied bombing. Her father had carefully schooled her in what she should do if bombs hit the building in which she was living. She was to take a specific route to one of the principal bridges, under which there was a shelter. One day, when the family was gathered together, bombs fell on the city. They all ran to the cellar for greater protection. A bomb hit the building, and she, being small, was lifted through the casement window to the street. She was told to run to the shelter under the bridge to wait for her family. She arrived safely, but they never came; the building collapsed killing her entire family.

A bright, intense young woman, her face was partially paralyzed from the injuries she had suffered in the attack.

But her psyche was almost irreparably damaged. She was intent on an unconscious search for her lost family, which she acted out in a sexual, hysterical, self-damaging manner. She could not tolerate closeness, acting out her conflicts in a manner that continually interfered with therapy. Finally, she drifted away from treatment and I have never heard of her again. Like many millions of children around the world, she was simply a victim of the time and place where she was born. The political implications of the incident were completely meaningless to this damaged child, who will likely suffer for the rest of her life.

The struggle to find meaning in the face of chaotic tragedy was powerfully portrayed by Arthur Miller in his play *After the Fall*. Holga speaks:

Quentin, I think it's a mistake to ever look for hope outside one's self. One day the house smells of fresh bread, the next of smoke and blood. One day you faint because the gardener cut his finger off, within a week you're climbing over the corpses of children bombed in a subway. What hope can there be if that is so? I tried to die near the end of the war. The same dream returned each night until I dared not go to sleep and grew quite ill. I dreamed I had a child, and even in the dream I saw it was my life, and it was an idiot, and I ran away. But it always crept onto my lap again, clutched at my clothes. Until I thought, if I could kiss it, whatever in it was my own, perhaps I could sleep. And I bent to its broken face, and it was horrible . . . but I kissed it. I think one must finally take one's life in one's arms, Quentin.[4]

What Elie Wiesel learned on the eve of Rosh Hashanah and Holga learned in the story from the play is the first and greatest lesson for sufferers. That is, "The suffering is mine!" This is the first task in making meaning from suffering, to look at its terrible face and own it as belonging to ourselves. This acceptance of mortality, ownership of our own imperfection, recognition of our own aloneness in the world, is the beginning of whatever recovery is possible. It opens the way for us to seek God for ourselves, to recognize the value of relationships, to understand how much we *need* the support of our friends, our families, and our faith.

Meaning-making as a Vital Necessity

In the long run it doesn't matter whether the causes of suffering are just or unjust, individual or corporate, understandable or chaotic; the unavoidable personal task is to put life back together, making meaning of the environment within which it is lived, and go on from there. This requires one to evaluate and accept the reality of the problem, to take the "idiot child" of one's awful situation on one's lap, embrace it, and own it as being one's own. The volume of feelings is important at this point. To choke feelings off may require defensive maneuvers that will permanently impede emotional freedom and intellectual power. To allow feeling to spill over unimpededly and repeatedly may deepen helpless and dependent feelings, resulting in a permanent loss in control and intentionality. The support and control offered by medical, psychological, or clerical professionals can be very useful at this point.

The second, and more difficult and important task for the sufferer, is to rework the meaning structures of life into new, acceptable, perhaps even satisfying, configurations. Such a reworking of meaning structures, which may include both beliefs and relationships, can result in a richer and more satisfying life. Several of the persons described in this book such as Mary, Sinclair, Ted, Sarina, Miss Martin, and Aunt Betty have had considerable success in doing this.

The Conditions for Meaning-making

Certain conditions are needed if we are to survive the crises of suffering. They will directly affect our ability to reorganize and make sense of our situation and will determine the success we have revising our meaning structures. Some of the important factors to be considered are the following:

1. The nature of the onset of the crisis. The more unexpected and debilitating the crisis the greater the possibility of confusion followed by long-term complications. Those of you who have experienced bereavement will likely agree that the death of a loved one is more manageable when

there is a fairly long "warning" period. Long illnesses provide an opportunity for pre-grieving and adapting life's structures in advance of the loved one's death. Changes in living arrangements and financial matters can often be gradually adjusted. Such illnesses also give the opportunity for recognizing and understanding changes in our status and relationships. Gradual aging also allows such an adjustment to take place.

However, when major crises come without warning, all of the resources of the person's life support system are called upon: family, friends, religious groups, and caregiving professionals. Abandonment, the sudden death of spouses or children, unforeseen financial catastrophes, sudden losses of employment, or sudden critical illnesses are such crises.

2. Prior success in life management. We are all in training for the unexpected crises of life. The normal separations of life are preparations for permanent losses of loved ones. Our children do leave home to be on their own, love affairs do terminate, good friends do move away. All of these are "mini-deaths" that serve us in good stead when bereavement comes. The success with which we manage these is important preparation. The same may be said for the daily practice in time and money management. And understanding our bodies' limits and learning to employ good health-care practices are the best preparation for the unexpected limits that may occur during severe illnesses. In all these respects, major crises will not seem so discontinuous from the rest of our lives, or as overwhelming as they otherwise might be.

3. The nature of our remaining options. This is an important modifier of the experience of suffering. One of the most important steps for Sinclair, as he was recovering from Guillain-Barré syndrome, was to discover that he had many untried options left, despite some permanent changes in his physiological limits.

It is important to take stock. What do we have left after the disaster? Our lives must be reshaped not only to take into account new limits that may have been forced upon us, but also to take full advantage of elements in our personal repertoire that have never been fully employed. Invalids are often good listeners. They have compensated for limitations in mobility by becoming more sensitive to the vibrations around them. Highly developed social sensitivity and communication skills can sometimes open doors to new vocational opportunities.

4. The nature of one's support community. There are usually some surprises in store in this area. It is important to learn the difference between the Marys and the Marthas when a crisis occurs. That is, between those who speak of support and understanding, and those who are prepared enough, and committed enough to stick with the relationship for the long haul. There is a time when sitting at the feet of someone is less helpful than providing practical care that helps people carry on with life. Hence, new relationships often need to be made. These may include support groups specially devised to bring together persons with problems like our own. We may learn the value of physical therapists, alcohol counselors, rape support groups, bereaved parent groups, prayer groups, or many other forms of support in battling back from crises. Within one's own family structure some surprises may occur. We will disappoint ourselves if we expect family members to become dramatically more mature or caring because we are in crisis. It is important to learn to evaluate and fully use one's support community.

5. The completeness and flexibility of one's value system. Crises of suffering may require that new ethical and moral choices be made. Our decisions may need to be deeper and more clearly focused. Some of the rigidities we could afford when we were "well" may be unimportant in a crisis of suffering. We may not be able to maintain the same safety from ideas and behaviors that are different from our own. Privacy may be harder to maintain. We may be called on to make decisions about the extent and severity of methods of treatment. A crisis of suffering may turn life into a "Vale of Soul-making," to use John Keats' analogy.[5] As theologian Paul Schilling has explained, Keats' view was a

classic formulation of the teleological type of theodicy. According to this view, life, in the purpose of God, is a school of character formation, a training ground for the growth of moral personality. The sufferings encountered are valuable instruments for the fashioning of mature men and women.[6]

Many of us who would not agree with this "classic formulation," that is, that God allows suffering to come our way for the good of our souls, can still see the value of turning potential tragedies into experiences of learning and growth. When we face and answer the tough questions of life it surely broadens and deepens our moral-ethical "reference library" so that we know how to behave with appropriateness and grace in the face of very difficult circumstances. It will be no secret to the reader that I believe that the value questions facing a sufferer can best be worked out within the framework of a well-understood Ultimate Context. For most of us, whose Ultimate Context includes a belief in God, our suffering occurs within the framework of God's love and care.

6. A willingness to change. Sufferers who can accept the probability that life will never be the same again are helped. This does not mean that life will be worse—it may be better than ever—but it will be different. Suffering often offers a new, wider ranging view of human experience. It makes one more aware of human mortality. It tends to shift values about. Some things become dramatically less important than they always were, while others take on new meaning. This may result in changes in friendships, avocations, conversational topics, reading material, and religious practices. In this sense, suffering is like getting married: One should expect to change.

All of these are factors that will affect the success with which we can not only endure suffering, but also use it as an instrument for our growth. Whether or not we grow through suffering depends on what I earlier referred to as "prodromal ego strength." Healthy-minded approaches to life work for healthy-minded people.

I visualize a certain unknown threshold of ego strength above which suffering strengthens, and beneath which it destroys. Persons who enter the experience of suffering with weaker self-structures need more help if they are to survive. To both survive suffering and to reshape the meaning of life so that there are residual benefits from the period of suffering may require study, psychotherapy, group work, or a deepened religious awakening.

It seems unnecessarily self-referential to believe that suffering has been designed specially, to test our mettle or enhance our growth. I do not believe that the Holocaust and other events I have mentioned were part of a divine plan to test the mettle of human beings. They were senseless acts of calculated or wanton violence. Nevertheless, we as sufferers are faced with the meaning-making task. From Job to the latest victim of thoughtless crime, the unanswerable questions are often, How did I get this way? and, Who's responsible? But the more relevant questions are, What do I do now? and, How do I get it done? In this direction lie relationship, growth, and mastery.

Knowledge for the Future

We can be warned by tragic events against the unqualified power of governments and their leaders, and against our own errors, mistakes, and stupidity. We can learn not to take too many chances, not to trust too quickly, to keep machinery (human and otherwise) in good repair, and not to be too much on our own.

Most of the illustrations I have used were derived from the suffering of persons who have experienced tragic "acts of God." That is, accidents, illnesses, losses, and bereavements. But for the great body of sufferers such incidents are only further explications of a continual state of suffering. Those who suffer from war, prejudice, poverty, and oppression are by far in the majority of sufferers. Statistics provide a clear record: If a person is born poor, black, in a Third World country, or female, there is an additional possibility of suffering with each of these variables.

The most valuable lessons to be learned from suffering are lessons for the future. We should learn to value human life, to see how infinitely precious is each single human being. We should learn that the role of government is to enhance the value of human beings by extending human life, underwriting creativity, and providing humane care of the helpless and suffering. We should learn that our bodies are precious temples of spiritual life, that they should be protected from harmful drugs, abuse, and assault. We should learn that every moment is precious, to be savored and cherished, never to be rushed through. And we should learn that life hangs by a slender thread. We are sensitive mortal creatures capable of great sins and great inspiration. We have the exceptional gift of being able to derive creativity and beauty from every realm in which we live, whether it be the ash heap, the ghetto, the gas furnaces, or our own death beds.

If we are indeed made "a little lower than the Angels" and "in the image and likeness of God," then we can be sure that, although the suffering is ultimately ours alone, God knows our pain and expresses this knowledge through the caregivers, called to do the work of healing, who stand in the place of God.

Notes

Chapter One: The Nature of Suffering

1. Kurt Koffka, *Principles of Gestalt Psychology* (New York: Harcourt Brace and Company, 1935), pp. 27-28.

2. Charles E. Osgood, *Method and Theory in Experimental Psychology* (New York: Oxford University Press, 1953), pp. 410-12.

3. Sigmund Freud, *New Introductory Lectures in Psychoanalysis,* (New York: W. W. Norton and Co., 1933), pp. 90-91.

4. Dietrich Bonhoeffer, *Letters and Papers from Prison,* ed. Eberhard Bethge, trans. Reginald H. Fuller (New York: Macmillan Paperbacks Edition, 1971), pp. 146-47.

5. Ibid.

6. Friedrich Mesmer, *De planetarium influxu.* Reference taken from E. G. Boring, *A History of Experimental Psychology* (New York: Appleton Century Crofts, 1950).

7. Ibid., pp. 120-21.

8. Harry S. Sullivan, *The Interpersonal Theory of Psychiatry* (New York: W. W. Norton, 1953), p. 262.

9. Ernest Becker, *The Denial of Death* (New York: Free Press, 1973), pp. 50-51. Copyright © 1973 by The Free Press, a Division of Macmillan, Inc. Reprinted by permission of the publisher.

10. Stanislas Breton, "Human Suffering and Transcendence," in *The Meaning of Human Suffering,* Flavian Dougherty, ed. (New York: Human Sciences Press, 1982), pp. 60-61.

11. Russell R. Monroe, "Integration of Psychoanalytic and Other Approaches," in *The American Handbook of Psychiatry,* Silvano Arieti and Eugene Brody, eds. (New York: Basic Books, 1974), p. 214.

12. Norman Cameron, *Personality Development and Psychopathology* (Boston: Houghton Mifflin, 1963), p. 263.

13. Teilhard de Chardin, *The Future of Man* (New York: Harper & Row, 1964).

14. Ana-Maria Rizzuto, *The Birth of the Living God* (Chicago: University of Chicago Press, 1979).

15. Paul Tillich, *Systematic Theology Volume 1* (Chicago: University of Chicago Press, 1951).

16. De Chardin, *Future of Man.*

17. Simone Weil, "The Love of God and Affliction," in *Waiting on God,* (London: Routledge and Kegan Paul, 1951), pp. 64 ff.

18. Dorothee Soelle, *Suffering* (Philadelphia: Fortress Press, 1975); see chapter 1, "A Critique of Christian Masochism," pp. 9-32.

19. Eric Cassel, "The Nature of Suffering and the Goals of Medicine," *The New England Journal of Medicine* 306 (1982): 643.

20. *Webster's New Collegiate Dictionary* (Springfield, Mass.: G. & C. Merriam Co., 1977).

21. Anna Freud, *The Ego and the Mechanisms of Defense* (London: Hogarth Press, 1937).

22. N. R. F. Maier and J. B. Klee, "Studies of Abnormal Behavior in the Rat, VII. The Permanent Nature of Abnormal Fixations and Their Relation to Convulsive Tendencies," *Journal of Experimental Psychology* 29 (1941): 380-89.

23. M. Kovacs and A. Beck, "Maladaptive Cognitive Structures in Depression," *The American Journal of Psychiatry* 135 (May 1978): 525-33.

24. Søren Kierkegaard, *Fear and Trembling and Sickness unto Death,* trans. Walter Lowrie (Garden City, N.Y.: Doubleday Anchor Books, 1954), pp. 144, 150.

25. Lee Meyerson, "Somatopsychology of Physical Disability," in W. M. Cruickshank, *Psychology of Exceptional Children and Youth* (Englewood Cliffs, N.J.: Prentice-Hall, 1955), pp. 1-60.

26. Bonhoeffer, *Letters and Papers.*

27. Alan Paton, et al., *Creative Suffering: The Ripple of Hope* (Philadelphia: Pilgrim Press, 1970), p. 15.

Chapter Two: The Quality of Suffering

1. Leo Tolstoy, *My Confession and the Spirit of Christ's Teachings* (New York: Thomas Y. Crowell, 1887). The quotations that follow were taken from *The Varieties of Religious Experience* by William James because the language lent itself to contemporary understandings more than did the earlier translation from the Russian published by Crowell. James appears to have translated the material from a French translation by "Zonia." James abridged some of the passages. See footnote, p. 135, *Varieties of Religious Experience* (New York: Collier Books, Macmillan, 1961). The passages are taken from pp. 133-35.

2. D. S. Browning, *Religious Ethics and Pastoral Care* (Philadelphia: Fortress Press, 1983), p. 58.

3. I. D. Yalom, *Existential Psychotherapy* (New York: Basic Books, 1980), p. 355.

4. M. Kovacs and A. Beck, "Maladaptive Cognitive Studies in Depression," *The American Journal of Psychiatry* 135 (May 1978): 525-33.

5. See E. Erikson, "Identity and the Life Cycle" in *Psychological Issues* vol. 1, no. 1 (New York: International Universities Press, 1959).

6. Tolstoy, *My Confession,* pp. 133-35.

7. George Santayana, "Orbiter Scripta," *Lectures, Essays, and Reviews* (New York: Charles Scribner and Sons, 1936), pp. 170-71.

8. Sigmund Freud, *New Introductory Lectures in Psychoanalysis* (New York: W. W. Norton, 1933), p. 82.

9. Ruth Munroe explains Sullivan's term "dynamism" on p. 357 of *Schools of Psychoanalytic Thought* (New York: Henry Holt, 1955).

10. Ernest Becker, *The Denial of Death* (New York: Free Press, 1973), pp. 3-4.

11. Carol Gilligan, *In a Different Voice* (Cambridge: Harvard University Press, 1982).

12. H. Kohut, *The Analysis of the Self* (New York: International Universities Press, 1971).

13. Heinz Kohut and Ernest Wolfe, "The Disorders of the Self and Their Treatment," *International Journal of Psychoanalysis* 59 (1978): 413-25.

14. H. S. Sullivan, *Conceptions of Modern Psychiatry* (New York: W. W. Norton, 1940), p. 22.

15. D. H. Buie and G. Adler, "Treatment of the Borderline Patient," manuscript (Boston, 1979).

16. René Spitz, "Anaclitic Depression: an Inquiry into the Genesis of Psychiatric Conditions in Early Childhood," *Psychoanalytic Study of the Child* 2 (1946): 313-42.

17. A. Rizzuto, *The Birth of the Living God* (Chicago: University of Chicago Press, 1979), pp. 87-88.

18. C. Rogers, *Client Centered Therapy* (Boston: Houghton-Mifflin, 1951), p. 503; and H. S. Sullivan, *The Interpersonal Theory of Psychiatry* (New York: W. W. Norton, 1953), p. 161 ff.

19. Becker, *Denial of Death*, p. 55.

20. James, *Religious Experience*, p. 134.

21. David Roberts, *Existentialism and Religious Belief* (New York: Oxford University Press, 1957. Galaxy ed.), p. 117.

22. Erich Fromm, *The Sane Society* (New York: Rhinehart, 1955). In all, Fromm mentioned five normative human needs: relatedness, transcendence, rootedness, identity, and a frame of orientation.

23. Abraham Maslow, *Motivation and Personality* (New York: Harper and Brothers, 1954).

24. Carl Rogers, *Client Centered Therapy* (Boston: Houghton Mifflin, 1951), p. 489.

25. Ibid. The quotation from Andras Angyal is taken from Angyal's book *Foundations for a Science of Personality* (New York: Commonwealth fund, 1941).

26. Teilhard de Chardin, *The Future of Man* (New York: Harper and Row, 1964).

27. Rogers, *Client Centered Therapy*.

28. James, *Religious Experience*, p. 135.

29. Geoffrey Bromiley, *Introduction to the Theology of Karl Barth* (Grand Rapids, Mich.: William B. Eerdmans, 1979), p. 142.

30. C. Kegley and R. Bretall, *The Theology of Paul Tillich* (New York: Macmillan, 1961), p. 160.

31. Bromiley, *Karl Barth*, p. 142.

32. Ibid.

33. Mwalimu Imara, "Dying as the Last Stage of Growth" in Elisabeth Kübler-Ross, ed., *Death: The Final Stage of Growth* (Englewood Cliffs, N.J.: Prentice-Hall, 1975).

Chapter Three: The Many Faces of Suffering

1. Robert White, *The Abnormal Personality* (New York: Ronald Press, 1956), p. 209.

2. Søren Kierkegaard, *Fear and Trembling and the Sickness Unto Death* (Garden City, N.Y.: Doubleday Anchor Books, 1954).

3. Eric R. Kandel, "From Metapsychology to Molecular Biology: Explorations in the Nature of Anxiety," *American Journal of Psychiatry* 140 (October 1983): 1277-92.

4. Charles Osgood, *Theories of Learning* (New York: Oxford University Press, 1953). See pp. 392 ff.

5. Sigmund Freud, *New Introductory Lectures in Psychoanalysis* (New York: W. W. Norton, 1933). See chapter 4, "Anxiety and Instinctual Life."

6. J. R. Greenberg and S. A. Mitchell, *Object Relations in Psychoanalytic Theory* (Cambridge, Mass.: Harvard University Press, 1983), pp. 93-94.

7. J. B. Calhoun, "A Behavioral Sink," in *Roots of Behavior*, E. L. Bliss, ed. (New York: Harper Hoebner, 1962).

8. Paul Tillich, *The Courage to Be* (New Haven, Conn.: Yale University Press, 1952), pp. 35-36.

9. Ernest Becker, *The Denial of Death* (New York: Free Press, 1973), pp. 50-51.

10. Tillich, *Courage to Be*.

11. Colin Murray Parkes, *Bereavement: Studies of Grief in Adult Life* (New York: International Universities Press, 1972).

12. John L. Maes, "Loss and Grief in Fathering," in *Fathering: Fact or Fable?*, ed. E. V. Stein (Nashville: Abingdon, 1977).

13. Ibid.

14. Sigmund Freud, "Mourning and Melancholia," *A General Selection of the Works of Sigmund Freud* (London: Hogarth Press, 1973).

15. H. Akiskal and William McKinney, "Overview of Recent Research in Depression," *Archives of General Psychiatry*, vol. 32 (March 1975), pp. 285, 291.

16. Marie Kovacs and Aaron Beck, "Maladaptive Cognitive Structures in Depression," *The American Journal of Psychiatry* 135 (March 1978): 55.

17. Karl Menninger, *Whatever Became of Sin?* (New York: Hawthorn Books, 1973).

18. See Kovacs and Beck, "Maladaptive Structures."

19. Hobart Mowrer, *The Crisis in Religion and Psychiatry* (Princeton: N.J.: Van Nostrand, 1961).

20. Teilhard de Chardin, *The Phenomenon of Man* (New York: Harcourt Brace Jovanovitch, 1974).

21. Mwalimu Imara, "Dying as the Last Stage of Growth," in Elisabeth Kübler-Ross, ed., *Death: The Final Stage of Growth* (Englewood Cliffs, N.J.: Prentice-Hall, 1975), p. 149.

22. Elaine Scarry, *The Body of Pain* (New York: Oxford University Press, 1985), p. 4.

23. Heinz Kohut, *The Restoration of the Self* (New York: International Universities Press, 1977).

24. See S. Snyder, *Madness and the Brain* (New York: McGraw-Hill, 1974), pp. 215 ff.

25. R. Melzack and P. Wall, *The Challenge of Pain* (New York: Basic Books, 1973), pp. 27-28.

26. Ibid., p. 222.

27. Ibid.

28. Scarry, *Body of Pain*, p. 7.

29. Ibid., p. 8.

30. N. C. Andreason, *The Broken Brain* (New York: Harper and Row, 1984), pp. 180-81.

31. Ernest Jones, *The Life and Works of Sigmund Freud* (New York: Basic Books, 1961), p. 529.

32. *Diagnostic and Statistical Manual of the American Psychiatric Association* (Washington, D.C.: American Psychiatric Association, 1987), p. 316.

33. Freud, *New Introductory Lectures*, pp. 89-90.

Chapter Four: Overcoming Despair

1. Edwin Arlington Robinson, "Richard Cory" in *Prose and Poetry of America* (Chicago: L. W. Singer Company, 1934).

2. See chapter 1, page 34.

3. William Cullen Bryant, "Thanatopsis," from *American Prose and Poetry*, Forester et al., eds. (Boston: Houghton Mifflin, 1970).

4. Maya Angelou, *Singin' and Swingin' and Gettin' Merry like Christmas* (New York: Bantam Books, 1977).

5. A Rogerian term widely used by client-centered therapists. See *Client Centered Therapy* (Boston: Houghton Mifflin Co., 1951).

6. Ernest Becker, *The Denial of Death* (New York: Free Press, 1973).

7. Anna Freud, *The Ego and the Mechanisms of Defense* (New York: Hogarth Press, 1937).

8. Becker, *Denial of Death*, pp. 51-52.

9. Victor Frankl, *The Unconscious God* (New York: Simon and Schuster, 1973).

10. From John Bunyan's *Pilgrim's Progress*.

Chapter Five: Responding to the Sufferer

1. See *Anticipatory Grief*, Schoenberg, et al., eds. (New York: Columbia Press, 1974).

2. John L. Maes, "Loss and Grief in Fathering" in *Fathering: Fact or Fable?*, ed. E. V. Stein (Nashville: Abingdon Press, 1977), p. 107.

3. H. Zimmer, *Myths and Symbols in Indian Art and Civilization*, ed. Joseph Campbell (New York: Harper and Brothers, 1946), p. 8.

4. H. Hartmann, ref. found in D. Rapaport, *Organization and Pathology of Thought* (New York: Columbia University Press, 1951).

5. Paul Tillich, *The Courage to Be* (New Haven, Conn.: Yale University Press, 1952).

6. K. Lewin, *Principles of Topological Psychology* (New York: McGraw-Hill, 1936).

7. Primary narcissism is a term used in psychoanalytic theory and refers to the child's early libidinal attachment to his or her own body. This pre-object attachment stage is normal for little children, but pathological when it appears in later life.

8. M. Jordan, *Taking on the Gods* (Nashville: Abingdon Press, 1987).

9. M. Imara, "Dying as the Last Stage of Growth," in *Death: The Final Stage of Growth*, Elisabeth Kübler-Ross, ed. (Englewood Cliffs, N.J.: Prentice Hall, 1975).

10. Ibid., p. 159.

11. These ideas were first presented in a symposium at the Harvard Club in Boston and were published in a chapter titled, "Maturity, Spirituality, and Suffering," in *Maturity and the Quest for Spiritual Meaning*. See n. 7, above.

12. Victor Hugo, quoted in *The New Book of Christian Quotations*. Compiled by Tony Castle (New York: Crossroad Publishing Co., 1983), p. 50:C346.

Chapter Six: Suffering and Meaning

1. Elie Wiesel, *Night* (New York: Bantam Books, 1960), pp. 63, 64.

2. Ibid., pp. x, xi.

3. Ibid., p. xi.

4. Arthur Miller, *After the Fall* (New York: Bantam Books, 1965), pp. 30-31.

5. M. B. Forman, ed., *The Letters of John Keats*, 4th ed. (London: Oxford University Press, 1952), pp. 334-35.

6. Paul Schilling, *God and Human Anguish* (Nashville: Abingdon, 1977), p. 147.